Printed in the United States of America

Cover Design: Claire Last

Luminare Press
467 W 17th Ave
Eugene, OR 97401
www.luminarepress.com

ISBN: 978-1-944733-02-5
LCCN: 2016950345

Volume I

LIFE
SPARKS

LIFE STORIES TO
ILLUMINATE, INSPIRE AND IGNITE

COMPILED BY
Tami Blodgett & Denise Beins

LUMINARE PRESS

WWW.LUMINAREPRESS.COM

Contents

Introduction

Welcome to Life SPARKS—overflowing with sparks of inspiration!

Within the pages of this compelling book, you will meet the authors who are real-life "sparks of inspiration." Through candid, dynamic and dramatic stories, they share a passion that creates positive change in the world—right here, right now. Each author relays a message that is profound and diverse. One story won't fit all, but among all of the stories, *at least one will especially fit you!*

Their stories reveal a *life spark* that ignited from a single incident—resulting in an unexpected, personal transformation. This book draws from a plethora of backgrounds, experiences, fears and tears—with no two alike.

We are honored to represent these gifted people, because it allows us to fulfill the purpose of our business, which is to empower others to live out and express *their* individual purpose as they share their message.

In the Life *SPARKS* programs, we support authors by coaching them through the process of writing. They publish and share their personal story in a safe and supportive community. At the same time, contributing authors are prepared about how their story, and who they are, complements their business—which in-turn allows them to be readily known, seen and heard by a broader audience.

Now we invite you to grab a hot cup of tea or coffee, sit back in a comfortable chair, and join us on the journey. You can look forward to experiencing a transformation right along with our authors, where you will then go on to *illuminate, inspire and ignite* someone else.

We want to thank our authors, not only for being vulnerable in sharing their stories, but for digging deep within themselves to uncover the true meaning of the experience, and the profound effect it had on shaping their lives today. It's our hope that by the light they shed on a subject, something challenging is exposed, helping you to recognize that "certain something" that may be festering quietly deep within yourself. May the *sparks* in this book shed a glimmer of hope on the challenging emotion or situation that is revealed to you—further inspiring you today.

Our goal? Our greatest desire is that you are renewed in ways only you know. Our purpose is for you to move forward, and more readily feel equipped to take action. We are confident these short stories will ignite something dormant inside of you that has been waiting for this *spark* of inspiration.

Are you ready? We are, so please turn the page.

Tami Blodgett and Denise Beins

"BEAUTY OF WHATEVER KIND, IN ITS SUPREME DEVEL-
OPMENT, INVARIABLY EXCITES THE SENSITIVE SOUL TO
TEARS."

—EDGAR ALLEN POE

Reclaiming Your Gifts Of Sensitivity

CATHERINE VANWETTER

"You're just too sensitive." "I can't tell you anything without you crying." "Why are you so thin skinned?" Those words as a young child were seared into my psyche. I began living them as if they were the truth of who I was and what I was to become. As a result, my life long journey has been to learn how to reclaim my beautiful self and proclaim the magnificence of who I am—fully accepting the large part of me that lives out each day being a "Highly Sensitive Person."

I remember as a small child, my parents letting me know that what I was feeling was not accurate—that somehow what I was sensing was not okay. Yet, I continued to feel and sense things that many didn't. I could feel the angst of someone in grief, somehow knowing that they weren't doing well. Yet, when I voiced my knowing and concern, it was blocked out with silence, rebuttal or "Buck up. You're too fragile. You're too intense. You're too thin skinned. If you don't change, I'll find a way to break you." I became confused as a child and disoriented in a world that invalidated my deep knowing, my sensitive self.

As I reflect back, my environment as a child was harsh. My parent's doing the very best that they could, didn't know how to interact with a child that was so sensitive. Due to their own childhood, and not having resolved their wounded upbringing themselves, having a sensitive child reminded them of emotions that they were *not* comfortable dealing with. As I have looked back at the photos, I see a child that was lost and confused; somehow trying to make sense of a world that was lacking sense. My eyes looked dull and empty, and my smile was fake. I learned that what I felt was not valued. Today, it's painful to see.

As a young child, I remember laying in bed at night and listening to the coyotes as they wailed and sang to each other. As scared as I was at the thought of them, somehow, I felt solace in their cries. It was as if they were voicing my own sorrows and grief that I had no way of expressing. They became my constant companions—my allies, my witnesses and my safe haven.

I grew up in the high Sierras, and would spend hours by myself hiking, running, crying, playing music—feeling connected and embraced by the silence. Nature never hurt me. Only people did. Somehow nature melted away my angst and helped make everything okay.

Discovering a way to find peace, solitude, refuge, and something bigger than me helped me to feel grounded, enabling me to let go of my intense feelings of being alone in a world that felt so hostile. Releasing my emotions through crying, seeking the comfort of isolation, and the loving companionship of my dog, helped me to find ways to fit into a world where I felt so by myself and misunderstood.

Because I didn't know how to be in the world as a

sensitive, I became clever, and took on the form of being a chameleon, a ghost, a shadow of what I thought others wanted me to be. I learned how to blend in, how to be a pleaser, how to not be a burden. In the process, I lost my sense of self. I lost my identity, my voice and my integrity. I had learned early on that, my sensitive self was an embarrassment—a part of me that was somehow not accepted and therefore should be discarded. Yet, as hard as I tried to have a "thicker" skin, I continued *to feel* the world around me and would often collapse from the weight of all that I took in that wasn't mine—rather it was absorbed from the people and life around me. I had difficulty separating my feelings and emotions with others. This created panic attacks, anxiety and depression—even though I was too young to have a word for it.

A trauma that haunted me for most of my life was the loss of my younger sister, when I was seven and she was four. She had leukemia and died six months after she was diagnosed. My parents, dealing with their own stress and anxiety, never let me know that my sister was dying. Yet, I knew. She would come home from the hospital where she was receiving medical treatment on the weekends and I knew that she wasn't well, yet they kept their silence. She died two days before Christmas. All my mother said was that she was a star. I never went to her funeral and never said goodbye. She was not spoken of after that.

Life after her death became tense; emotions were high. I suffered from anxiety, depression—without help and totally on my own. As a way of coping, I became bulimic. My parents overcome in their grief, didn't know how to address this, and so I continued to numb my feelings with food. I left home at the tender age of seventeen, hoping to find a place with people who could help me feel safe and take care of me. I also hoped that my parents would reach out and welcome me back into their lives. Neither happened.

After leaving home, I became a vagabond. I stayed with friends and moved around a lot looking for a safe place to land. Not until I raised my own sons did I realize how young we are at seventeen. I flashed back on my own life at that age and how afraid I was to be out in the big world. Feeling so alone and inexperienced—with a heart that felt heavy and so sad.

I found ways to support myself financially, but just barely. It felt like I was always on the edge of despair, picking up minimum wage jobs or spending the summers picking fruit and playing music. I found a way of coping. I also delved into alcohol and drugs; anything that would help numb my intense feelings about my highly sensitive self. I remember always wanting to go home. What I recognize, now that I am older, is that I wanted to go home to myself—to feel safe and satisfied with my highly sensitive self.

Always trying to fit in, my continuous internal, unconscious inquiry was, "Who do you want me to be? I can be that person." People pleasing tossed me every which way. Each time that I evolved into another "person" another persona, I sacrificed and lost more of my authentic self. After a while, I had no voice—no "backbone" to be who I was destined to be.

I continued using drugs and alcohol as a way to "feel normal." It numbed out my intense feelings of being so alone, my way of wanting to forget who I was and what others thought of me. When I was twenty-four, I had my first experience of suicidal thoughts. My heart hurt so much not knowing where I belonged. By this time, my parents had disowned me—and feeling so despondent and lost, I believed that taking my life would free me from the pain.

Yet, time after time, something so much bigger than me, kept me here on this earth. I'm not sure what that was other than my resilience, resourcefulness and the deep, profound knowing that Spirit had a bigger plan for me, insisting that *somewhere* and *somehow* my life had meaning and purpose that I had not yet realized.

I began spending my life searching, becoming more educated, taking endless workshops and being in countless relationships that led nowhere. I felt like a "hollow" body— empty of sustenance, of value, of self-esteem and worth. I was smart, intellectually, yet did not inhabit my body. Life became a burden—for me, a mere human doing nothing more than going through the motions day-in and day-out.

Finally, on my knees once again, I consented to the reality, that it was *not* my time to go, nor my time to exit life. With that profound, yet daunting recognition, I began to realize that my sensitivity to all the people, events and things around me was, in fact, such a beautiful and precious gift. Slowly, I began accepting how I was wired. The question then became, *how do I move forward in a healthy and balanced way as a sensitive?*

Through spiritual counseling, meditation, and education in the area of highly sensitive people, I began focusing my attention on creating clear boundaries with myself and others, practicing impeccable self-care, and with curiosity and gentleness, exploring what it meant to be a highly sensitive person. I gave up escaping with alcohol and drugs, worked on self-forgiveness, compassion and gratitude as a way to fill my "hollow' body *from the inside out.* I recognized that *it was not the outside world that harmed me, rather the continuation of self-deprecation that kept me a victim of my wounded self-perception.*

I have continued to slowly, gently and patiently, embrace my sensitivity. I recognize that it is a lifelong process and being diligent is important. Every day I am reminded of my vulnerability and my commitment to stay true to my calling of being kind, generous and loving to those who may not see or feel the world as I do. It has become my endless practice.

Being *sensitive* enables me to notice the gentle sweetness of life. *And at last,* I can appreciate that sensitivity to all and everyone around me is a blessed part of my everyday life. In doing so, I find more sensitives drawn to me, and I to them. I'm not the only one!

And I also recognize that my purpose is to kindly remind those who have lost their way, raising my awareness of honoring *who* other people are, and in doing so, perhaps I help them to acknowledge and accept their authentic self.

We are all deeply interconnected. My sensitivity is also my passion, work and responsibility. It is a way to guide those who have forgotten or buried their true self in harmful thought patterns and behaviors—causing them to stumble and temporarily lose their way.

It is with tremendous gratitude, that I can now wholeheartedly say, that I am grateful that I was born as a highly sensitive person. What a beautiful gift and blessing it is.

I leave you with this poem I wrote…

From the Eyes of a Sensitive

From the eyes of a sensitive, my world looks different
than yours.

My eyes are filled with the beauty, magic and
elegance of the rising sun or the delicate
dewdrop hanging precariously from a leaf.

My heart is filled with the sorrow, grief and
unspoken fear that is somehow absorbed from
the stranger's eyes that I, for an instant looked
into.

My mind is full of unending possibilities, ruminating
rhetoric and visions of uncertainty. I have been
told that I'm too sensitive, too thin skinned, too
fragile and too intense. In the past, I took those
words to heart and wore them as if they were
the truth.

It led to depression, addiction, anxiety, suicidal
thoughts and isolation.

As I have been embracing, embodying, integrating
fully my sensitivity, I have found that it is my
greatest gift.

I am a visionaire, mediator, peacemaker and
moderator.

I am compassionate, open-hearted, vulnerable and
courageous.

I am the light of the future, the harmony of the
world and the healing of the soul.

As I use the "I"… it is the universal eye through
which we all see. I am you and you are me. We
have one heart, one breath, one mind.

Catherine VanWetter

Catherine VanWetter is a spiritual and shamanic practitioner focusing in the area of highly sensitive people. She holds a Masters in Social Work and is trained in multiple modalities such as Family Constellation Work, NLP (Neuro Linguistic Programming), HeartMath, mediation, couple's communication, positive discipline and sacred ceremony/ritual. Catherine is the author of two books, one of which is a best seller. She has hosted and been a guest on several inspirational internet radio shows—is a speaker, whose goal is to help others overcome adversity and increase compassion with sensitivity and love. Catherine feels, "I am humbly grateful to all of the teachers, mentors, guides and spiritual counselors who helped me find my way. As I have made peace with my sensitive self and honored those who came before me, it has enabled me to love all of me. My words and story now becomes my medicine. Catherine works with individuals, groups and families. Currently, she is hosting a BlogTalk radio show called "Authentic Messengers." She is also a contributing author of the *Life SPARKS book series*. She lives in beautiful Langley on Whidbey Island, Washington… home of the bunnies.

CatherineVanWetter@gmail.com

www.GiftsOfSensitivity.com

"Our deepest fear is not that we are inadequate. Our deepest fear is that we are powerful beyond measure. It is our light, not our darkness, that most frightens us..."

—Marianne Williamson

No More Excuses—
Open Your Doors of Discovery

SUSIE BRISCOE

Who am I? To do such and such—or to be gorgeous or talented—thoughts like these, of self-doubt, haunt many women, perhaps all women at one time or another. We can liberate ourselves—to shine brightly, and learn to not feel self-conscious about so doing.

How? Well, my unshackling of insecurities began through charity volunteering, bringing with it some unexpected surprises. Doors opened, many of which, historically, I would never have dared to even try to open.

More importantly, I found out how my efforts in charity work could impact the lives of women around the world. Through it, I discovered the delight and satisfaction of giving of oneself. It's the answer to becoming more fulfilled, gaining skills and confidence, as we share of our individual gifts and light. Knock on any door—I want *you* also to discover—it will open!

I can still remember how strange it felt. I was about to make my debut speech. Did I want to share the stage with celebrities in front of an audience of six hundred—many of the *great* and *good* of English society? No! Not if I was in my right mind. Ummm…?

It was a magnificent occasion—The Egyptian Hall, in London's Mansion House, home to The Lord Mayor of London. This venue receives esteemed guests, from Her Majesty, The Queen of England, exalted international celebrities and U.S. presidents. What on earth was I thinking?

This great public adventure wasn't something that I'd really thought through—because someone else always stood up front, certainly not me.

A little back story: My dear friend, the late Sir Greville Spratt, had been elected Lord Mayor of London—an historic title dating back to 1189. (We met when our children had attended the same preparatory school.) Interestingly, the people who comprise this ancient list, reveal just how many were everyday citizens, merchants and grocers, similar to you and me! Feeling lack in my own ability and standing, I wish I had known at the time that "the list" of historic Guilds had been set up by the aspiring working/middle class. They are proof that the contribution of oneself has a fine history, started by ordinary people who want to make a difference in the lives of others.

I had *(almost)* innocently asked Greville, "Please, may I have 'The Mansion House' for a day?" I requested this on behalf of the charity we both supported, "Action Medical Research." It funds vital medical research, with emphasis on difficulties in pregnancy and much more. If he agreed to the use of this magnificent House, I had fully expected Greville or his darling wife, Sheila, to happily take the public lead. He duly came back with permission, and we started planning a medieval-style English 'Fayre' to be held in the grand rooms of the Lord Mayor's *cozy* little home. *Mm-hmm…*

So, on the morning of our fundraising fair, I awakened in a bedroom inside the House itself, fearfully thinking *who am I to speak in front of these people?* Regardless, I soon stood next to the late and great Millicent Martin, whose career had begun alongside David Frost, when they were both starring in the iconic 1960s television show.

'Millie' had convincingly hugged me into fronting it with the microphone. (My best friend—*Uh-huh!*) She was absolutely marvelous, whispering encouraging words of support to calm me, as I stood like wood, awaiting my turn, which was upon me right after the Lord Mayor finished speaking.

My speech only took two minutes—yet those minutes were purgatory for me. My mouth was, so dry I had to stop to moisten it, so she thought I'd finished... embarrassingly, I had to whisper that I still had more to say. *Arghhh...!* The anxiety of waiting, the trauma of having such a daunting audience, the sheer number of people attentively listening before me was mind-blowing.

None too soon I left the stage, and my friend and vice-chair, Gill Cribbins—wife of the veteran actor/film star Bernard—was there to catch me. She said, "It went well!" I was in shock, my heart was pounding—but yes, we had pulled it off.

With emotions abounding, I thought of how we had very nearly managed to persuade Michael Jackson, who happened to be in London at the time, to come. At this instant, I was so grateful he was not in the audience for my awkward speaking debut. But uh-oh, I then remembered, renowned singer, Eartha Kitt was there—who, upon her arrival acted very *diva-ish*, though in retrospect, she probably just didn't know where to go or what to do. We imagine celebrities are different than us, but they're just people—with insecurities like everyone else. I know that now, years later.

All-in-all, the event was a huge success. Without realizing it, there was a change in me: I had found my mojo... *no more excuses* allowed! We had turned 'Mansion House' into a medieval-themed fair in the broadest sense; including organ grinder, but no monkey—the poor little monkey had been banned from the get-go by Sword Bearer, one of the grandly-titled gentlemen who attend to the Lord Mayor—*Awww...!*

(Learn more: https://en.wikipedia.org/wiki/Lord_Mayor_of_London)

We overcame our want of the monkey—with fabulous activities upstairs, in the Salon, and throughout the many reception rooms. There, fairground archetypes dressed in tried-and-true period costumes—stilt-walkers, colorful clowns, including Harlequin and Pierette, jugglers, a circus ringmaster, stalls selling a variety of goods, amongst a smorgasbord of other marvelous delights.

But — once again, we were thwarted — first no monkey, and then we were not allowed fire-eaters *(Sword Bearer, at it again!)* Can you imagine our disappointment?

We were kindly reminded that this was to be the first public showing of the multimillion pound Samuel Wallace art collection, gifted to the grand Home of The Lord Mayor of London. But still, remind me: why not allow the fire-eaters? *Oh dear...!*

All was not lost, as Bill Pertwee, the English actor/film star made the extraordinary announcement at noon: "You have passed the £100,000 mark in monies raised today." (Exchange rate: £1.00 = 1.15 US Dollar)

We went on to raise a total of £155,000! Quite a feat, considering our first attempt at a remote location in the country raised a mere £1,100. Our efforts to raise much needed funds for our charity had been exceeded.

Why am I sharing this story with you? Because if someone like me, an ordinary, everyday housewife living in a little country lane, can contribute to such an occasion by standing up to speak in front of grand London society, then you, too, can do something equally as daunting!

The driving force is a personally important "why," propelled by "you"—your personality and passion. Each of us has different reasons that drive us forward, giving purpose, helping to form a plan—energizing us to move mountains and achieve seemingly impossible tasks.

"Dream no small dreams for they have no power to move men."

—Johan Wolfgang von Goethe

Allow me to share from deep within. I alluded earlier that I had personal reasons for choosing to support Action Medical Research, with its emphasis on difficulties in pregnancy.

The doors I knocked on, and those you will knock on and open, involve work that is personally driven, a desire of the heart. My passion for helping women with difficulty in pregnancy was the result of the disappointment and pain of my own miscarriages—ten in total. These losses came one after the other—very nearly losing my first baby—who gratefully—has grown into my beautiful, 44-year-old daughter, Lara.

There is something very defining, if not sobering, about

being pregnant— few things match the fear of knowing you may possibly lose your baby, dashing your hope for a child.

As you would expect, both my husband and I were excited at the prospect of our first child; however, we faced the thought of losing her early, at the three months' stage of pregnancy. The shock was beyond belief. I prepared to do whatever it took to ensure her safety.

Fortunately, doing as my gynecologist directed—staying on bed rest—held my first baby safely intact up to seven months, until I had to be admitted to the hospital on complete bed respite.

Pre-eclampsia, and endless other complications forced an early delivery at thirty-six weeks. Having to be induced, then laboring long and hard, an emergency cesarean section ultimately had to be performed. During my postpartum check, I learned that I had ticked all the boxes for high risk pregnancy. This again made me realize just how blessed my husband and I were to be holding Lara in our arms, watching her sleep, or listening to her sweet sounds. Each time she cried, or I changed her nappy, was a gift of life.

Looking back at the miscarriages after Lara, I remember feeling I had two choices: 1) Throw in the towel; despair, give up and feel sorry for myself that I was miscarrying all my babies after Lara; or, 2) help raise funds for research which might benefit other women and families.

You guessed it! Taking on the role of a victim, choosing to live life feeling sorry for myself would wear *very* thin on me and those around me. In that decisive moment, acceptance and appreciation for Lara's birth, and the joy she bestowed upon me, guided me towards volunteering with "Action,"—which required patiently waiting, because to volunteer locally was by invitation only.

To quote Lewis Caroll's Walrus, in the *Alice in Wonderland* books, I decided that "The time has come…" and so it was that my working in the voluntary sector began with a gentle, yet ongoing, vengeance.

The door had opened for me, and so did a completely new world—*without excuses*—bringing with it remarkable gifts of personal learning, and increased understanding of how both the challenging circumstances and new accomplishments of today are merely a prelude—preparation and promise—to help us through future moments tomorrow.

The word 'destiny' comes to mind. It's an interesting one; for me, I believe that there is a guiding light which leads and protects each of us. Some call this Spirit, God, Divinity, fortune, chance, providence, lot, or luck.

You may not be religious or overtly spiritual, but whatever you feel comfortable with, I encourage you to embrace this sentiment from outside ourselves—although in truth, I do believe that whatever 'it' is called, the result is the same. We are all treasured, comforted and protected by the same force the world over. Through this, we learn *about* ourselves and learn *how to be* ourselves—on stage and off!

> *"Not being able to do everything is no excuse for not doing everything you can."*
> —Ashleigh Brilliant

Susie Briscoe

Susie Briscoe is the Founding Chair—International Business Executive Coach, Mentor and Master Leadership with Legacy Mentor: "Helping Professionals and Business Leaders find Rainbows within their Lives."

Susie founded Acer Coaching Associates (ACA) in 2004, after graduating as a fully accredited coach, mentor and supervisor with Coaching and Mentoring International. Her cutting-edge practices attracted the attention of Nightingale Conant and Brian Tracy International, leading her to become their freelance Master Coach outside the US. Susie runs her international business while remaining active on several charity Boards in the UK, her home country.

An enthusiastic corporate and executive motivator, Susie is fervent about facilitating the developmental growth of clients and colleagues. Her coaching style has been described as intuitive, empathetic, compassionate and motivating.

Since implementing her own Leadership with Legacy ideas, Susie joyfully declares her intention of "Finding the rainbows in all those business suits." Truly, nothing is more pleasing to her, than to hear the delight in client's voices as they too discover and believe in their own skills and passions.

briscoe1@freenetname.co.uk

www.acercoachingassociates.com

"As we become purer channels for God's light, we develop an appetite for the sweetness that is possible in this world. A miracle worker is not geared toward fighting the world that is, but toward creating the world that could be."

—Marianne Williamson

An Unexpected Awakening

ANITA C. STEWART, R.N.

My back was broken, my legs numb. Lying in the hospital bed, I pondered the recent series of troubling events. What had happened to my life? One minute I was living the life of my dreams, and the next I was unable to move my legs. No one could have ever told me events would play out this way.

My husband Mike and I thrived on our ranch with two horses and two dogs, in the hills north of Los Angeles. I had a great job working as an ER nurse, and selling real estate part time. Mike, formerly an LAPD officer and now a real estate agent, was my partner. We were living the American dream. Then, fate reared its ugly head and our dreams came crashing down.

Interest rates spiked to 21 percent, killing the housing market. With our real estate business in the tank, Mike took a job as a security guard to help make ends meet. Our income was outpaced by the never-ending bills—our stress soared! Thank God, we found solace riding our horses in the vast openness of nature.

One morning, while putting on my riding boots, I had a premonition; a vivid movie in my mind showed me being dramatically thrown from my horse. Clearly, I saw a "county" medevac helicopter land, but since we lived in the "city," I ignored this vivid premonition.

We began our ride into the hills, with the horses energized and raring to go. As we rode onto a wide open trail, we let them run at a full gallop. In his excitement, my horse bucked, the most spirited buck I had ever experienced, pitching me head first onto a rock. I felt my back snap, and immediately lost feeling in my legs.

Unable to move, Mike ran to my rescue. Luckily the horses ran safely to a nearby ranch, causing the rancher to ride out looking for us. Due to the severity of my injuries, helicopter transport was required. As it landed, my eyes were drawn to the "County of Los Angeles" insignia. *My earlier premonition had come true.*

I was flown to the nearest trauma center, Northridge Hospital, where I also worked. The exams, x-rays, and scans revealed that I fractured my back at the T-12 vertebrae; I also fractured my skull and left scapula, (the hardest bone in the body to break). During my two-week hospital stay, rehab was intense. To even budge, required large quantities of pain medication.

Arriving home, I needed help with just about everything. Four long arduous months, barely moving from the bed to the recliner—recovery took all the physical and emotional strength I could muster.

One day my nurse buddy, Margie, visited. She was a spiritual seeker. At work, we talked about spirituality, God, and consciousness. She brought me a book to read called, *Quiet Talks with the Master* by Eva Bell Werber. After

Margie left, I felt so alone; with the annoying "ticktock" of the grandfather clock the only sound.

I'd never read this type of book, but began to read, and my anger swelled—why hadn't I heeded my premonition? Why were we losing everything we had worked for? I glanced at the chapter heading, "Be Still and Hear my Voice."

I screamed out loud, my negative early-childhood experience with "religion" feeding my anger. "Okay God, if you want me to listen to you, make that clock stop ticking." Abruptly, the clock went silent. The pendulum kept swinging, but there was absolute silence.

Then I heard His voice. A loving voice filled with palpable energy. "My child, you have so many questions. I am here to answer them."

What? God is talking *to me!* My mind was filled with questions, but even before one was fully formulated, the answers came.

His voice continued, "You must learn to keep this stillness, to retreat into it whenever confusion arises in your physical or mental world. Thus shall all difficulties solve themselves, by *my power* working through you. Learn to 'be still' instantly, and watch *my power* work."

As God knew, my worries were many; financially, we even borrowed money to put gas in the car. I heard, "You need not worry, child, all this shall pass. Stay ever-present on Me, my voice, and walk this day forward in trust and faith." I sat there—*in awe.*

Time stood still. My head, filled with these personal answers from God, brought me comfort and relief. I wasn't alone. My worry evaporated. A gentle, unexplainable peace came over me. I *trusted* this voice.

Even with all the challenges facing us, I had confidence

that nothing would rattle me from here on out. I called my husband and said, "Mike, God just spoke to me and we have nothing to worry about."

He thought the skull fracture had made me crazy. But something inside me *knew—everything* was going to be okay!

I felt blessed beyond compare! In an instant, it was abundantly clear; I was here to do God's work, using His healing energy through my hands. "How?" I asked. He answered, "All you need to do is get your ego out of the way and the work will be done through you."

"Don't I need to study or take classes in order to *understand what to do?*"

"NO!" He sharply answered, "You need only show up. Allow the energy to pass through you like a conduit. The healing will be done by My power."

In the days following this *unexpected awakening*, I did nothing on my own volition. Tuned-in and listening, I heard His voice directing me in every situation.

It was so fascinating, having this sudden ability to innately know what was to come—to be able to hear God's voice as clearly as if He was speaking to me in person. The feeling was surreal, reality of His presence simply flowed.

We wanted to sell before foreclosure, but interest rates were too high. There were no buyers; our payments fell further behind. I was guided to create "for sale" fliers. Handing them out at a horse show, I met a man who, out of the blue, bought our property at asking price.

After four months of rehabilitation, I returned to my job in the ER. Mike was hired as a paramedic. We sold our house, the horses, and most of our possessions. We found a house to rent and slowly got back on our feet.

I continued heeding God's guidance, which brought clarity and peace to my life. When God spoke, I listened. It was not hard. I was told to buy a healing table and invite friends over to experience this *energy work.*

I had no personal energy healing experience; I was intuitive, and as a child, I healed birds with broken wings and other animals. Perhaps I was intended for this work—and God knew what I didn't. I had no idea what to do, but by now I was trusting His voice and moved confidently ahead.

My friend Rachel, also a nurse, was my first guinea pig. As she lay on my table, my movements were not of my own; I was guided by an unseen spirit. Although skeptical at first, she said she experienced an intense heat coming from my hands. As my hands were hovering over her pelvis, I stated, "Rachel you have endometriosis!" (Later confirmed by her doctor.) The day after the healing session, she called and said, "My period began at 2:00 a.m. this morning!"

And so it began. There were many amazing results from this healing energy work flowing through me. With complete trust and faith, I just showed up. I let go and surrendered to Divine Intelligence—that knew where and what was needed.

Confirming messages came through for clients. It was as if this unknowable force was speaking using my voice... the words just flowed. Now, for over 35 years, lives touched by this energy work keep me in deep appreciation and wonder.

The words of others humble me. "She pushed me through my self-inflicted limits..."—"Beyond any expectations..."—"I've been really high ever since..."—"I feel super relaxed and low stress..."

Profound changes occur: fears are overcome; lifestyle

and relationship changes; no further need of medications—all too numerable to list—and unexplainable in human terms.

Then suddenly, after eleven months, *silence!* The voice was barely discernible. I felt the bubble had burst. Speaking one more time I heard, "These things I do through you, you too can do. But first you must do the inner work."

I felt empty, devoid of ability or direction. But this undeniable experience ignited a passionate search for more answers, like those inner truths that had been freely given. An unimaginable journey to re-discover this *great mystery* was set in motion.

Today I have utter peace, unshakeable faith, and a life filled with grace and wonder. This awakening returned me to innocence; a child comfortably at play amidst the mysteries of spirit and consciousness.

By giving up all that I held as true, my limited beliefs and control about how things are "supposed" to be, I have come to a place of "knowing." What I know is, "You can't put God in a box."—it's both as simple and as complex as that.

Aligning with the mind of God, receiving Divine Intelligence, requires complete and unmitigated surrender. Only in our silence can we come to know the truth.

As time went on, I wondered how I could embody the gifts from this journey going forward in my life. Learning to listen, to discriminate, and to practice this love I had experienced—and to not live in fear, were daily lessons.

Entering into silence through meditation, I learned to relax and release my ego. Looking beyond appearances and personalities, I feel gifted to see what lies beneath. It was Emerson who said, "What lies behind us and what lies before us are tiny matters compared to what lies within us."

Today, I have a growing practice in Bend, Oregon, "Bridges of the Heart." It is said, "The longest Bridge a man will cross is from his head to his Heart." It is my greatest passion to help bridge the way into a life filled with unconditional acceptance, turning everything one gravels with, into a gateway to a deeper understanding of our Essential Nature (and oneness).

As one becomes receptive to a grace deeper than the mind, extending to the heart, one moves into the boundless *heart of being—where* one discovers we "are" that which we seek. The transformations I am honored to experience with people fill *my heart* with abundant joy. Working with them, I am *reawakened*—I am blessed.

Anita C. Stewart, R.N

Anita C. Stewart, R.N. has been gifted to work in healing her whole life. Earnest tending to those injured was first experienced through her compassionate, gentle care of animals as a child. She went on to earn her nursing degree, with high level hospital nursing as her career for 40 years. Her own debilitating injury initiated a series of events that naturally led her to expand her abilities to help others, physically, emotionally and spiritually—not through her own knowledge and power, but through surrender to a power greater than her own. Energy healing, at times and for some, is unexplainable in words, but seen in the transformed lives of those through whom Anita provides her specialized care. Her holistic approach utilizes hands-on energy alignment, with the goal of bridging Energy Medicine into mainstream medicine. Naturally intuitive, she identifies areas in need of work and guides patients through a journey of deep self-discovery.

www.bridgesoftheheart.com

www.facebook.com/bridgesoftheheart

"Death has taught me the magic of life, how precious each moment is and how living in the NOW is the key to happiness. There is no death, there is only transformation."

—Petra Nicoll

Comatose

PETRA NICOLL

Veränderung! Change within me.

December of 1970, one of the coldest winters Bavaria had seen in years, dropped temperatures to twenty degrees below zero. We lived outside of Munich, Germany, in my hometown of "Markt Schwaben," which was covered by a blanket of shimmering snow.

The plows could barely keep up with the heavy downfall, which greatly amused us children always ready for the next adventure. To us, it was a magical winter wonderland. I was nine years old, dreamy-eyed and full of youthful play and laughter.

My mother had warned me to stay home and take care of my cold, but life was too exciting, and I insisted on spending the night at my fun aunt and uncle's. Their apartment was cold, and I coughed until my ribcage ached, sending shivers running down my spine.

When I got back home, my mother bundled me in a cozy blanket on the sofa, and in her sweetest voice, kissed my forehead, and played some soft classical music. Encouraging me to swallow some "good" medicine down, she then left for town with my brother, Wolfgang, for a quick, urgent errand. I slowly drifted to sleep.

Out of the blue, I woke up with such terror, jumping in panic. Desperately gasping for air, I sounded like a barking seal at the circus. I flailed around as my cough worsened.

Between coughs, a strange crow-like noise escaped me—a wheezing sound like the one my friend made when she had an asthma attack. I could feel my chest sink with each gasping breath. Something wasn't right! I touched my ribs; they felt displaced.

Barely, conscious, my body shifted and jolted in spasms again.

Out of dazed desperation, mustering all my strength I stood up, and raised my arms above my head, frantic to open up my air passages so I could breathe. Each time I attempted to breathe inward, my airways tightened even more. I finally gave in.

Suddenly, everything turned quiet and still, like the snow outside.

A beautiful humming filled my ears—it was peaceful and quiet; fear and terror left me. I fell to the floor and rolled under the glass coffee table. The chest pain stopped. I began drifting toward a bright light—not of this world. I slipped out of consciousness, withdrawing from my body.

Time passed… My mother's voice called, "Petra!" She pulled me from under the table. Once again, I felt the unbearable tightness in my chest as I gulped for oxygen. She screamed at Wolfgang to keep me upright, commanding him to walk me around the house. In my delirium, I almost fell down the stairs. My poor brother! Immediately, Mother called for my dad to drive us to the nearest hospital in Steinhoering, a town 15 kilometers from us.

At 14-years-old, my mother had been hospitalized there. She had contracted the polio virus and was paralyzed for two years. The worst part, besides the pain, my mother said, was the emotional ache of being locked away there. Unable to hug her own mother, except through a dingy, institutional window, made her feel like a prisoner.

No air to breathe.

Later, I would learn this about the hospital— its' roots in dreadful Nazi evil.

In 1935, a feared Nazi, Himmler, created a secret Nazi program called "Lebensborn" in this hospital. Deemed racially pure, young women were taken from their families and isolated in those cavernous walls to *meet* SS officers, to bring "racially pure" into the world. Nazi authorities believed that these Lebensborn children would be purebred Aryans, perfect future SS-leaders (given to the SS to train from birth); the new nobility that would dominate the world. At least, that was the plan. (Ref. https://www.jewishvirtuallibrary.org/jsource/Holocaust/Lebensborn.html)

I knew none of that at nine years old. Instead, I felt light and peaceful, in a state of altered consciousness. Not in my body, I floated upward, hovering on the hospital ceiling, not in my bed, which felt strange.

During this experience, I witnessed my body from a distance, its every move, *my Spirit* moved along the walls of the old hospital.

How was this possible?

"What is happening to me?" I faintly recall asking.

I watched from above my body. My father stood down there next to me, holding my hand close to his heart, his tears falling on my lifeless face. I could feel his sadness and aching heart. I knew he didn't think I was going to make it.

Maybe this was a part of the Steinhoering legacy, the giving and taking of innocent lives. Yet, I wasn't worried. I wasn't "Petra" in her hospital bed; I was hovering above them, an observer.

My mother, in her red fox coat, sat in the dank corridor. She was on a bench, reading something, black pen in hand, her face pale. She appeared numb with dismay, a horror no mother wants to endure. Somehow, in my out-of-body state, I knew she was signing a document to consent to a dangerous surgery.

I remember thinking… *Poor mummy, watching me on the edge of death in the same dreadful place she had to remain while ill in her childhood.*

Momentarily, I felt as if I was slipping into her body, mind and spirit—I could feel her sorrow and despair. Her intense emotions came over me in a vibration of dread and sadness.

I then *traveled* into an operating room, where two doctors in their light green, baggy scrubs, and several nurses, vigorously scrubbed and washed their hands. I had a bird's-eye view. Wherever my attention focused, there I was. I could see clearly. I felt what everyone was feeling, as if I was able to slip inside their bodies and read their minds. Experiencing their every emotion, didn't seem odd or scary; I felt calm and neutral, unemotional, as I moved through the corridors.

I remember trying to get their attention, thinking I had called out to my father, "Pappi, Pappi—I'm up here!"

Then I said something like, "Don't cry—I'm alright, you don't have to worry about me." I continued, "I'm up here, I'm up here—look up, I am on the ceiling!! I am fine!"

But my Pappi stared at my lifeless body and couldn't hear me calling out.

What is happening to my spirit? Why is my body lying there, yet I am on the ceiling looking down at my body with such a sense of calm?

I recall feeling this inner knowing that everything was perfect on those cream-white walls, when, suddenly, my spirit shot through a tunnel much like a vortex of clouds, illuminated by a bright white light.

I was flying like a bird, up, up through the sky. I felt this strange energy project me through the light with such enormous speed. It was as if I was enveloped by this brilliant ray inside and out. The sun was hugely magnified. I felt safe. It was otherworldly and intoxicating to my spirit.

I eventually found myself in an edifice that appeared like a gigantic library with a multitude of floors and books reaching into the vast sky. The joy, love and peace prevailed inside me. Feeling free and incredibly warm from the inside out, the humming sound reverberated throughout this tall library.

It all seemed strangely familiar.

In an instant, I stood next to seemingly wise old men. They reminded me of the ancient Babylonians, dressed in simple cloaks of white and brown, or the Franciscan monks in Bavaria.

One had a hefty, old book in his hand. He read from this leather-bound book. As I stared at their handsome, weathered faces, I felt like I had known them before, and they knew me. I felt I recognized one man in particular. He had the most peaceful and kindhearted face.

There was a bluish light emanating from him, and his eyes were so blue and bright that I wanted to get lost inside of them. I recognized Jesus the instant I set eyes on him. I could not conceive of a more loving face and eyes. Jesus and the other elders were talking about my fate, united in their care and concern. We were ONE.

They weren't talking like humans talk. Their conversation–telepathic; I could somehow perceive their thoughts and deep messages of love.

Not a little girl anymore, I felt timeless and *one* with them. No identity, no borders—I felt truly at home in their affection, their compassion.

I asked them if I could stay. But, no...

They smiled at me the way a loving father smiles at a daughter.

And then—all went black.

The following morning, I woke up in the Intensive Care Unit in a huge room with old, wooden floors. There was only one other young child, in a meager crib—with a strange mushroom-like growth on his mouth.

His abnormality frightened me. I closed my eyes so I didn't have to see it. Now, awake, I felt the pain and suffering in this old hospital that reeked of rotting wood and iodine. The peace I had just experienced—gone—and I didn't like it.

I looked away from the child, and heard the *creak* of a heavy door, like that of a medieval castle. High-heel shoes echoed down the corridor—and then, the familiar voice of my mother.

I could barely make out what she said: "Herzilein, Herzilein, you made it; I could not live without you!"

She kissed my face, and stroked my hair. My aunt held my hand; I tried to speak, but I couldn't utter a sound or open my eyes.

What happened? Why was I back and how long had I been gone? I had no idea.

My entire body was exhausted. Then it happened again.

The peace returned, as if God himself was holding me in his arms. It seemed I floated in a warm liquid, and the soothing, humming sound, like Tibetan chant, was all around. I was terribly sick, my mother still worried, but my trance-like state seemed to envelop me in such a deep bliss that I have very little memory of what went on around me for the rest of my recovery.

One morning at breakfast, not long after I returned home from the hospital, I told my mother about the light and about Jesus, when she gently put her index finger on my lips and said, "Shhhhhh… we will never talk about this; little girls don't talk to Jesus, and if you do they will put you away in an insane asylum."

Something unexplainable had shifted inside of me. I was changed, and felt strangely detached from my family, and my life as it was before. I wished I could go to the place of peace and love forever—*it* was home.

Petra Nicoll

Petra Nicoll is a Transformational Story Coach who helps clients live to their highest potential by asking, "How do lessons become positive, even in the midst of much darkness, despair and grief?"

Through the extreme tragedies she has experienced, including the death of her mother, suicide, depression, and realities of war, she became a "Seeker After Truth." She was led to The Masters of the Far East, The Shaman's of North America and Mexico, who woke her to the realization and vision that she has been given—to become transformed and more intuitive, authentic and soul-centered.

Petra studied Psychology and Art in London, has taught Traditional Usui Reiki and Emotional Processing to over 3500 Students world-wide. As an author, certified life coach, public speaker, entrepreneur, workshop and seminar leader she has facilitated hundreds of workshops with positive, sustainable transformations in individuals for over thirty years. Her passion centers around helping people reach their highest potential by clearing way emotional blockages that hinder them to move forward. She teaches simple ways to clear unresolved emotional issues through "Golden Light Meditation". Her memoir, *Petra's Ashes A Transcendental Journey*" will be released in the fall of 2016.

Learn more about Petra and her work at:

www.petranicoll.com

petranicoll@gmail.com

"I LOVE YOU FOR PUTTING YOUR HAND INTO MY HEAPED UP HEART AND PASSING OVER ALL THE FRIVOLOUS AND WEAK THINGS THAT YOU CANNOT HELP SEEING THERE, AND FOR DRAWING OUT INTO THE LIGHT ALL THE BEAUTIFUL AND RADIANT THINGS THAT NO ONE ELSE HAS LOOKED QUITE FAR ENOUGH TO FIND."

—ROY CROFT

The Truth Shall Set You Free

ED CONRAD

"For all time, I am loved and I am lovable. No exceptions." Early on, I experienced an inner shift that carried me away from this deepest knowing. As I share about separating from this essential inner truth—and my return to knowing and accepting love, you may be encouraged to do the same.

At two years old, I went with my family on vacation to Biloxi, Mississippi on the Gulf of Mexico, where I went to the beach with my two older sisters, Diane and Julie, my mother and Aunt Enie. After a morning playing on the beach, my mom and aunt asked my sisters to keep an eye on me while they walked to pick up some lunch nearby.

Thinking back on it, it was a bit unusual and risky, with my sisters only five and seven. But, that's what happened. When my mom and aunt returned with lunch, I wasn't there. They asked my sisters, "Where's Eddie?" Being that they were so young themselves and engrossed in their beach activities, they hadn't noticed that I had wandered off.

As my mom recalled over the years— she and my aunt

began to panic. Their eyes frantically searching the surf, they spotted my little bright blue bathing suit bobbing on the top of the incoming waves. They took off running toward me.

At almost the same time, a man nearby realized what was happening, and he also went running toward my bright blue bathing suit. He ran past my mom and aunt and got to me first. He found me unconscious, face-down in the water. Evidently the waves kept me from sinking. Quickly, he snatched my limp little body out of the warm gulf waters, and laid me down. Miraculously, this perfect stranger knew just what to do to begin to get the water out of my lungs, and then resuscitate me.

Who knows how long I had been unconscious. Once oxygen stops flowing to the brain, which causes blacking out, there is a three to six minute window to get the oxygen flowing again. Past six minutes or so, there is at least serious brain damage, if not death. How could I have known that these three to six minutes would end up being the most impactful three to six minutes of my life?

Fast forward thirty-three years. I still remember the date. It was Tuesday, August 5th. I was in my final year of seminary, and phoned my wife and best friend of fifteen years, as I had done almost daily. She and our daughter and son lived three states away. Together, we had decided it was best for her and our children to remain in our home town while I went to seminary. It wasn't long into our call when, without warning, I slid to the floor in shock and agony. She had broken the news, "I no longer love you; I want a divorce." It came out of the blue. I had no inkling and was devastated.

In the years that followed, similar painful separations

took place with women that I got close to. Ironically, I also found myself on the other end of this experience, when I ended my twenty-two year marriage, just a few years ago. She was devastated as well.

Recently, events of my life and the suffering associated with them reached a crescendo. It came to me to make a list of the most significant decisions, experiences, and events of my life—from age seventeen to the present day which had created pain, difficulty, or self-doubt.

I walked mentally and emotionally through time, year-by-year. The result? Sixty challenging and life-changing moments; unsettling on the one hand, and on the other, I realized it was healthy to acknowledge and purge, as I reviewed my plot mapping of forty-seven years.

All life events were woven together in an emotional, neurological web; a strong force for influencing my life—now, no longer hidden from me. "Here is the life I have created up until now," I said to myself. Clear insight began to emerge and soon I could see how all these moments in time were linked to the emotional impact little Eddie (me) experienced on that Mississippi beach.

I have learned: Not only did the event have emotional, psychological, and neurological impact, but the MEAN-INGS I attributed to this near-death trauma created a significant ripple through many nooks and crannies of my life. Those of us who have experienced emotionally charged moments as small children, subconsciously store rem-nants of these memories and meanings within our nervous system, and emotional awareness. Current brain science, including research into the "emotional brain" confirms this.

When life thrusts us into emotionally charged experi-ences as small children, the brain automatically grasps for what it all means. The conscious meanings we conjure up distort the truth, or, at best, reveal only part of the whole story. The impact of these meanings is life-changing.

Out of my young boy's undeveloped brain and awareness, I tried to make sense of a frightening moment, with meanings that became ever-present pivot points in my life. We all have done this in some way.

I uncovered these two meanings from little Eddie's inner world of meaning-making, which was greatly influenced by the fear and confusion experienced in Biloxi:

The women, who say they love me and are there for me, will abandon me. This is what I deserve.

When I venture out in life, be prepared that something really scary may happen.

I now know that my emotional brain has been locked into these meanings, and set to light up anytime that life appears to present these specific threats. Not only did the unconscious meanings I gave this single early childhood experience set me up for waves of fear in my relationships, they also showed up in a thousand various and vulnerable moments over the years—such as public speaking. I've done it lots, but I often have experienced a semi-suffocating type feeling, which, if put into words would be, "I'm scared of what might happen to me." I coped by shrugging it off or praying it away.

I am among countless numbers of us who have in some way managed to live at the effect of a child's self-made world. But, this kind of confusing and limiting web is never the measure of who we are. It is only a small shadow of who we are altogether, yet it has a disproportionate effect.

These two significant "meanings" I conjured up as a small boy about rejection and fear were just that, meanings that I conjured up. Neither of these meanings was real or true. Yet, because that was what I accepted and felt, I set the table for these meanings to play out in my life. It was not until my late thirties that I truly felt "safe and secure" with my mother. It was a very loving relationship from that time on, until her passing. Yes, the near death experience happened and it was frightening, but there was not a sliver of truth in the meanings I made up. That fact doesn't alter the outcomes of becoming wired for rejection and fear as a scared little boy.

The reality is meanings that we make up are just that— *meanings that we make up due to our own limited perspective.* Then, we mix these into a very sordid soup of assumptions. A relationship example: a man you love says, "I'm not in love with you anymore." Immediately, your meaning-making gremlins get to work. "I'm unlovable. He never really loved me. I'm too emotional. Once he really got to know me and my vulnerabilities, well, of course he would want to get away from me. Yes, all those odd little habits of mine would drive anyone away." And on and on. Sound familiar?

With all this said, there is a Renaissance taking place regarding treatment of childhood traumas. Until now, it has been widely accepted in psychology and psychotherapy that those of us who have passed through such things will live with irreversible effects. Granted, we can manage the effects, but the imprint of these experiences will remain. There is now clear evidence to the contrary.

As mentioned before, I had been experiencing chronic anxiety. Very near the time I took the inventory I referred to earlier, I was on a monthly Skype call with a group I'd been meeting with for several years. My concern about anxiety came up during the call, and I mentioned having done a forty-seven year inventory. I also mentioned that my list clearly pointed to my near-death experience as a boy.

The facilitator asked me if I had ever had a direct experience of that event. I said, "No. I don't consciously remember it. I was only two." "Do you want to have a direct experience of it?" she asked. I thought, *what does she mean?*

In addition to being a licensed psychotherapist, she was also a hypnotherapist and she was willing to lead me in a hypnotherapy session so that I could have a *direct experience* of what had happened sixty-two years ago. I hesitated and then agreed to go ahead with it.

So, she lead me into a realm of awareness that allowed me to access and connect with what lay behind the veil of conscious memory—and through the experience of being little Eddie that summer day on the beach at Biloxi.

Here's how the session went… I was walking out to the gulf waters, conscious of how mesmerized I was by all that water and the incoming waves. It was my first time to experience this. I walked right out into the warm water. It was fun and felt wonderful. Then, quite suddenly a wave came toward me and the water went right into my face. I sucked in so much water; I couldn't breathe or cry out. It was terrifying. Everything went blank.

Then, the next thing I was aware of—light—and feeling very scared. Opening my eyes, the first thing I saw was my mother kneeling in front of me, with a terrible look on her face.

When asked by the hypnotherapist, what I was thinking at that moment I said, "My mom looks so mad. She must be really, really angry with me! I must have done something really bad. Whatever just happened to me must have been my punishment!"

The hypnotherapist encouraged me to go ahead and feel my fright and my response to what I perceived as my mother's anger at me. After several minutes, she asked me to make a switch and become aware that there was another story about what was taking place there. She said, "Everyone there was very scared because they thought you would die. Everyone there loved you so much, especially your mom. She wasn't mad at you. That look on her face expressed her fear that she would lose you. Little Eddie, go ahead and let yourself feel all the love that was there for you in that moment."

My ending point is this: The "juxtaposition" of two very different accounts of what happened long ago, was only the beginning of the unwinding of my little boy's misunderstandings and the meaning-making which was born from them.

When I woke up the next day, after the hypnotherapy, for the first time in nearly a year, I felt no anxiety. And, such was the case the next day and those following. I felt sixty-two years of my fear—*of being left alone and unloved*—disintegrating. I could see and feel myself leaving that beach long ago being held in the loving arms of my mother.

So, now when I say to myself, "For all time, I am loved and I am lovable... no exceptions," I feel my heart opening to receive what has been true all along. May we all return to the truth of love.

Ed Conrad

Ed Conrad's roots are in Fort Worth, Texas and western Oklahoma. He received his bachelor's degree in philosophy from Montana State University and later completed his ministerial studies at Unity Institute in Unity Village, Missouri. Ed has served as minister and spiritual leader in communities across the U.S. He is the founding minister of Columbine Spiritual Center in Boulder, Colorado, and Unity in the Heart in St. Paul, Minnesota. He completed his ministry career in Eugene, Oregon, in 2013. His in-depth, forty-five year spiritual search and wide-ranging life experience have forged his passion for helping people free themselves of lifelong emotional conditioning so that they may live extraordinary lives. He authored in 2014 the acclaimed daily reader, *Heart Power: Inspiring the Courage to Heal and Love Yourself One Day at a Time.* For more information on Ed's writings and seminars, please go to:

www.theheartpoweredpath.com.

edwardeconrad@gmail.com

"THERE ARE ONLY TWO WAYS TO LIVE YOUR LIFE.
ONE IS AS THOUGH NOTHING IS A MIRACLE. THE
OTHER IS AS THOUGH EVERYTHING IS A MIRACLE."

—ALBERT EINSTEIN.

The Truth about Forgiveness: My Journey to Grace

ALI DAVIDSON

orgiveness is a funny thing. Well, maybe funny, isn't the right word. People frequently talk about forgiveness—and that it's not about condoning the other person's behavior, but about choosing to let go of something that stagnates within the heart—such as anger or hurt. They say love the person who wronged you; rise above it. And so many other—dare I say—clichés?

I've never been one to hold a grudge; I don't stay angry for long. Maybe that's because I yearn to connect with others, and staying angry seems counterintuitive to what I want, which is relationship.

Regardless, when others have talked about forgiveness as simply a choice to be made, I would get irritated. I've never fully understood why. I think partly because those who said they'd chosen to forgive later demonstrated emotionally, that in fact, they still harbored anger and blame. None of us can simply think to ourselves, *I forgive*, and have it be so. It's a process. My story of heart-wrenching betrayal taught me that forgiveness is not something any of us can *just do*—*simply decide, talk ourselves into,* or *think our way through.*

True forgiveness is the natural outcome of letting go, a process that takes time: learning to *let go of being right,* of *expecting something to change,* of *trying to control a person or situation.* It's allowing the process of grief (whatever type) to run its course, to the point of acceptance. Acceptance of *what is,* of *what happened,* of *what you thought would be*—that now, *never will be.*

But how do any of us know if we have truly forgiven? The signs are clear, beginning with inner peace. And for me, when I think of, or am in the presence of the one who has hurt me, I no longer experience the physical signs of tightness in my throat, quickening of my breath, the fluttering of anxiety in my gut, or the fear in my heart. I am at ease. In other words, it is wellness in my body, peace in my heart, and calm thoughts in my mind, that assure I have done the work of forgiveness. And that work takes time.

There is no right or perfect timing, nor can it be forced. I had tried to convince myself I had forgiven this betrayal, but until I finally experienced a sense of ease, when thinking of the person or circumstance, that rushed through my body like liquid gold, forgiveness hadn't truly happened.

And the other dilemma—we can forgive, but that doesn't mean we forget. And it doesn't mean that it doesn't hurt anymore. It simply means we no longer feel the need to make it right, control it, change it, or even understand it.

I came to truly understand forgiveness when I experienced the worst betrayal of my life—that of my best friend and, my now, ex-husband. You guessed it! A full-blown affair, right under my nose, for almost a year, between the two people I trusted and loved the most.

My mind reels remembering all this. My body memory of that fateful day—my racing heart and tense muscles—still lingers. But I no longer feel the pain or anger. I've accepted that which I will never understand—and that is okay. As time passed, I allowed myself to surrender, let go of missing my once closest friend. And slowly I found that I could say her name in connection with my life stories, without hurting. Sometimes I would actually laugh, and I'd be pleasantly surprised. It's weird how forgiveness allows us to do that. I wasn't sure how I could ever fully forgive, but a surprise "encounter" with her changed my life.

Before going ahead, I must backtrack. Twenty-five years ago, I met her at a PTA meeting. This beautiful, tall blonde woman shared her angry protest about our current discussion point. She both enthralled and intimidated me—a weird way to start a friendship, I admit, but we did.

She quickly became my best friend—a soul sister. We talked, we laughed, we cried. With our husbands and children, we spent time together: holidays, home-schooling, raising 4-H pigs, and more.

It was to her that I confided the angst in my marriage. The pain of rejection, lack of communication, of feeling disconnected. And there were many times, over two-plus decades of life and friendship, that she told me to leave him and that I deserved better. So you can imagine the depth of my pain and shock when I found out she and my husband were cheating—together!

I'll never forget the day I found out.

My husband and I had had a fight, one of many, but this time it was different. My inner voice was screaming, "He's having an affair." I didn't want to believe it and I had no idea with whom he was cheating. One look at our phone bill, told me the ominous truth. He'd been texting my best friend and talking with her over the last four days. I called her. She said, "We are just friends and he's been unhappy." I replied, "Okay, but you know I've been unhappy, too."

Something in her voice and explanation sent the alarm bells in my head tolling. Fear crept into my pounding heart. Nothing she said made sense. "Did you know he was leaving me?" I asked. And she said, "Yes."

After more bewildering discussion, I hung up and went back to the phone bills. That's when I saw that the texts went back eight months, from ten to fifty times a day. Even in the middle of the night, while I slept, he was sending pictures of himself. I need not say more.

I felt like I was spinning in space, in a foreign place. Nothing seemed real, nothing made sense. How would I find my way back to solid ground? My best friend! My soul sister! My confidante! She had stepped into my life, betrayed me in a way that had broken my heart. My marriage was over already, but this doubled the pain!

Their affair ended the day I found out, when I told her husband. She did all she could to save her marriage, and she did. Leaving her husband for mine was never her intent. So, why had she done it?

I cried a lifetime of tears. Something precious had been lost. I couldn't quit asking why she had done it. Yet all I could do was accept it, which felt like an impossible task.

Over the next year, I could hardly say her name without palpitations. I realized that twenty-four years of my life's memories included her, and it hurt to remember. What had I done to make her hate me? How could she lie to my face for eight months, pretending to be my friend?

During the time she was having the affair with my husband we saw each other every week. I helped with her son's wedding. Our two families were together at Christmas. As couples, we had dinner and hot tub. All that time, she and my husband were meeting publicly, kissing, texting, even when I was near.

Life moved on. Still, there was no way of really knowing if I had forgiven until I was in her presence—the person who hurt me. Through a series of small time delaying events, I ended up someplace I had not planned on being—and suddenly there she was. We made eye contact, and I could see the fear in her eyes followed by the smile of recovery. My body took over before I even had a chance to think, and I walked right up to her. We each said hello and then I asked one question. "Why?"

Her answer was that she was "screwed up" and that she'd been in therapy for over a year figuring it all out. I asked if she'd thought of me when she was having the affair and she said, "Every day." Hmmm…?

The whole thing was surreal. Her answers didn't explain, and it didn't seem to matter. This friend, with whom I'd shared all aspects of life, was standing in front of me for the first time in over a year—and I felt the years of friendship and love for her flow through me.

It shocked and baffled me, but I wasn't afraid, shaking, or angry. She said people were waiting for her, so she couldn't talk, and promised to call me; I then stepped toward her with open arms, my body moving of its own accord.

As we hugged, clinging to one another, we both started crying. Crying for what we'd lost, and crying with relief of confession and forgiveness. As we held each other, she whispered again and again, over and over, "I'm sorry." And

I whispered back, "I know and I forgive you."

As our tears flowed, I felt all the questions and emotional hurt drain out of me. I felt a warm glow in my heart as I released all the pain. In that split second, the grieving was done and forgiveness had happened. It was beautiful—so tender and divinely orchestrated. I knew that only Spirit could have contrived this meeting, and given me the opportunity to truly forgive.

As we stepped back, I told her I'd always known that once I saw her I'd forgive her, even though I had been devastated by what she had done. Twenty-four years of sisterhood, of love, of sharing our lives, just couldn't be wiped away. To try to invalidate all we'd meant to each other, would have discounted all of life that we'd lived through, enjoyed and learned about together. I wouldn't; I couldn't do that.

I asked her if there was anything I'd done to hurt her and she said, "No, you never did anything but love me." With those words, my own self-doubt was released.

She said she'd call, but never did. I was okay with that. I can't say that I still don't wonder at times what she's doing, whether she misses me. I still occasionally wonder why she did it. Thankfully, I no longer feel desperately sad or angry. Now it's just a soft question and the soft answer is—it doesn't matter. Life moves on.

When my heartfelt forgiveness occurred, I walked away from her feeling like I'd been given the most exquisite gift from God. I could sense the hand of Spirit in every word, every nuance, every touch, and I was filled with gratitude— for the experience—but even more for greater awareness of the durability and flexibility of the human heart. For the journey to forgiving grace, for the truth of knowing that I'm never alone, and for the pure miracle that is life itself.

Ali Davidson

Ali Davidson is a transformation coach and teacher who assists women in realizing their authentic, connected and empowered selves. She is the author of *It's Between You and Me,* a workbook assisting seniors and their adult children in creating a plan for the aging years.She guides women through the challenges that life presents, helping them to successfully transform as life demands. Ali says, "One thing we can always count on is that change is constant." She believes our challenges provide the opportunity to grow and move us towards whom we are ultimately meant to be. "The cocoon can be painful, disruptive, and chaotic," she says, "but the metamorphosis of a butterfly is worth it!" Ali's own life experience allows her to empathize with every woman's story. Skills offered through her "Butterfly Quest Retreats," provides much-needed tools. Ali says we are all capable of so much more than we can ever imagine! We just have to be willing to give birth to our greatness."

alidavidson7@gmail.com

www.alidavidsonlifeacademy.com

"To discover who she is, a woman must descend into her own depths. . . To discover who she is, a woman must trust the places of darkness where she can meet her own deepest nature and give it a voice. . . Weaving the threads of her life into a fabric to be named and given. . . sharing it with the women around her as she comes to a true and certain sense of herself."

—Judith Duerk

Loss of Innocence

AMY HINDMAN

In 1963, I was in fifth grade, and ten years old. It was the time of The Beatles, The Beach Boys, Roy Orbison, *To Kill a Mockingbird*, troll dolls and transistor radios. I bought my first Beatles forty-five record with my own allowance: "I Want to Hold Your Hand," and "I Saw Her Standing There" on the flip side.

My parents gave me a "TV Pal Uke," and I learned my first song, The Kingston Trio's "Tom Dooley," which had two chords. I played it *endlessly*, until my dad said to my sister, Betsy, "I think it's time to teach her a new song." Then it was *all* Beatles: Betsy on guitar, singing harmonies to my melodies.

My parents didn't like The Beatles initially, mainly because the first picture of them that we saw on the front page of *The Denton Record Chronicle* showed them sitting on a couch *with their feet on the coffee table*. Seriously? Something about my parents and feet on the coffee table: don't do it! As soon as I left home, I never had a coffee table that I didn't put my feet on.

My family lived at 2610 Crestwood Place; I had a blue JC Higgins bike with red saddlebags and white tassels. I rode my bike to school every day, picking up my friend, Karen, on the way. Tessie, my black cock-a-poo, kept jumping the fence and following me; I guess we finally gave up trying to put her back in the yard—she became my companion at Woodrow Wilson Elementary School, hung out by the bike rack, greeted me at recess, and was still there when school let out to walk me home.

One beautiful sunny day, we got back to our classrooms and the teachers were strangely *absent!* After a while, kids started screwing around, unsupervised and playing in the hallway. Then, a teacher came and told us to go to Mr. Brooks' classroom, which felt strange, as it was a sixth grade class, and we were sitting at someone else's desk. We were told to sit down and wait. Then it was *very* quiet. Finally, the loudspeaker crackled, and Mr. Spratt, our principal said, "President Kennedy has been shot." We were all dismissed to go home to be with our families. Everyone seemed to be walking around in a daze, like an eerie episode of *The Twilight Zone.*

When I got home with Tessie, the TV was on, and my mom and dad were crying. They had been watching "As the World Turns," when a CBS News Bulletin interrupted: "In Dallas, Texas, three shots were fired at President Kennedy's motorcade in downtown Dallas. First reports say that President Kennedy has been seriously wounded."

"As the World Turns" resumed. Then, another news bulletin: "From Dallas, Texas the flash—apparently official, President Kennedy died at 1:00 p.m. Central Standard Time—2:00 p.m. Eastern Standard Time—some thirty-eight minutes ago."

I'd never seen a news guy try not to cry before. Walter Cronkite kept taking his glasses off, and putting them on again, and off again. And it had happened in *Dallas*! We lived so close to Dallas. I felt horrible that this happened in the state where I lived.

There was something very unusual, I guess, about this national tragedy that had not been seen before: a nation grieving together, through television. The TV was on for weeks, it seemed, with the whole country watching this real live drama: the swearing in of President Johnson, like *immediately*, with Mrs. Kennedy standing by him, the funeral procession, and most memorable, little Caroline with John-John saluting the casket as it passed.

My mother was diagnosed with cancer that year, too, and she was in and out of the hospital. We were all heartbroken by this national tragedy, and our own personal one. Mom's birthday was November 25th, and she turned forty-eight the day of John F. Kennedy's funeral at Arlington National Cemetery.

The next year, my mother died of cancer in August. She was buried at Arlington National Cemetery, on Chaplain's Hill, where my father, a Naval Chaplain, would also be buried when he died—right around the corner from John F. Kennedy's grave. They both died in Texas, and they were both buried at Arlington.

I would be going into sixth grade, and got the teacher that I wanted, Mr. Brooks. I was late starting school, because we had to go bury my mother, and then Dad thought we should all go to the New York World's Fair—so we did that.

The world was different for me then; I was the only person I knew, besides my brothers and sisters, who didn't have a mother, and I was changed, never to be the same.

Two years later, we left the small world of Denton, Texas, my dad remarried, and we moved to Bangkok, Thailand. I had started the first two months of eighth grade in Texas, and then we left behind our stories, our community, our roots and my beloved Tessie, leaving huge chunks of our life and our identity behind.

Years later, when I was twenty-eight, living on Lopez Island in Washington State, I woke up one morning, sobbing because my mother had died seventeen years ago. The emotion was so raw, as if it had just happened. I could barely walk down the driveway to Wendy's home. My dear friend took one look at me and said, "What's going on?"

Wendy had done a lot of counseling, and she asked me if I had ever done the Gestalt therapy thing, where there are two chairs: I talk to my mother and then switch chairs, and she talks to me. I said, "No, I hadn't." I was willing to try anything; I couldn't stop crying. We got settled in her living room, and began.

She said "Tell me about the night your mother died."

"I remember the night of August 26, 1964. There was a huge thunderstorm, and I was awakened by the thunder. I heard something in the den, and got up. Everyone was up, and my dad was on the phone, calling my brother, Steve, who was in the Navy, out at sea. My mom died that night around midnight."

Wendy said, "What were you feeling?"

"Well, everyone was in their own pain and crying. My mom was *really* gone. I had prayed every night for a year, asking God to make her get better, to please let her live. I felt like the bottom fell out of my life; who was gonna' take care of me?"

I felt stupid talking to an empty chair where my mother was supposed to be seated, imagining her there. I was directed to be both Amy and my mother.

Amy: *"Why did you leave?"* I switched chairs.
Mom: *"I didn't want to leave. I loved you more than anything in the world."* Switched chairs.
Amy: *"You never talked to us about it. You never said goodbye."* Switched chairs.
Mom: *"I didn't want to burden you children; I wanted to protect you from the pain."* Switched chairs.
Amy: *"You couldn't protect us from the pain! We felt it anyway!"* And back and forth—yadda, yadda, yadda...

At one point Wendy asked, "What are you *feeling* right now?"

As I listened to my body, I put both palms of my hands against my forehead, lifted my knees to my chest, and made a sound I didn't recognize as coming from me. It was straight from my gut—

"Ahhhhhh..." The sound was foreign and sustained.

We stayed in the quiet for a while. Then Wendy asked: "Where are you?" My voice was barely audible.

"Here."

This began my journey into that little girl, who was now demanding to be heard.

During this period of my life, there were many vivid dreams, in which my mother came to me. In one:

Mom came back. I remember being in an attic in Denton, I think in a school. She looked beautiful; she came over to me, smiling, and pulled my head to her chest.

I stayed there for a while, then looked up at her face and said, "I've wanted to feel that for a long time."

She smiled and said, "I know."

When I awakened the next morning, I was filled with the presence of my mom. I *knew* I had just been with her. I carried that feeling with me all day long.

I went out to lunch with my best friend, Kathie, and in the restaurant, this song came on as I was telling her about my dream.

"When at night I go to sleep, fourteen angels watch do keep." I was stunned!

I had never heard this song *recorded*; I had only heard my mother's voice singing this to me at bedtime—many, many times. She sang it in both German and English.

During my therapy, I had written a song called "Prayer for my Child," in which I imagined my mother, expressing her love for me. One of the lines was: "I come to you through dream and lullaby."

I had just had the most magical experience of being with my mom; I *knew* I was really with her, and she was sending me messages through dream and lullaby!

As this gaping wound began to mend, and I retrieved parts of my soul, I healed, and the wound became a scar, and an essential part of who I am today. I was given a powerful gift that would expand my heart and soul.

Music has always been my most valued form of expression, and it is healing for me when I sing or write a song.

"My mother wasn't around when I turned twelve
She left this life and moved on to another realm
And now I believe that her leaving was part of the
*   plan*

That she was giving me such a love letting go of my
hand
And there's love and compassion everywhere I go
Through illusions of sorrow and pain, I somehow
know
And sometimes when I wonder just why I've been
born
I know that love has something to do with my path
on earth"

I prayed often "please don't let grief bury my song." We always have that choice, I guess; to become the wounded and stay broken, or to somehow manage to go within, get the help we need, and deal with the tragedies we face to truly heal.

Amy Hindman

Amy Hindman is a singer/songwriter, performing and recording artist of three folk/rock albums. Her early life in Korea, Texas and Thailand influences Amy's meaningful work—"Healing Music from the Heart." She performed with Burl Ives in 1993—has received songwriting awards, judged by Paul McCartney, Sting and Rihanna. Her song "Gandhi and King: Becoming the Dream," was endorsed by Arun Gandhi, grandson of Mahatma Gandhi. Jamie Sams, author of *Medicine Cards,* also endorsed her music. Amy's connection to others, and depth of feeling is evident in all of her writing—on the page and in song. Amy says, "My music is an expression of my journey on this earth walk, created through the challenges and blessings that have formed who I am today. As I ever expand, grow, and open to the mystery, I will not be the same tomorrow." "You are invited to go to my website for a free download of one of my award-winning original songs. Also hear interviews and music; read the lyrics.

amy@amyhindman.com

www.amyhindman.com/contact

"A WOMAN IS LIKE A TEA BAG—YOU CAN'T TELL HOW
STRONG SHE IS UNTIL YOU PUT HER IN HOT WATER."

—ELEANOR ROOSEVELT

A Wreck In Paradise

PAMELA COURNOYER

t happened on a sunny Thursday afternoon in Mexico. I was cruising down a spectacular stretch of the Yucatan highway. The air conditioner in my classy new BMW rental car was set on high. I was prepared to inaugurate the weekend with two bottles of expensive champagne, while staying at the luxurious Bahia Principe Resort–an upscale condo with amazing seafood–literally fusion with the sea, enjoying "los mariscos" and "el pescado," surrounded by the finest local tourist attractions in all of Mexico. My client would be arriving in a few minutes, and I'd be ready for her. My coaching weekend intensive, *"Leaders in Paradise"* would begin that afternoon and last for three glorious days.

I was driving in heavy traffic, and the road became an obstacle course of parked cars. Noisy, local buses were loading and unloading passengers. Overloaded bicycle carts littered the spaces in-between. Anyone who has driven in Mexico knows the drill: senses are heightened, your eyes dart left and right, all serving as chaotic reminders that the typical gringo rules of the road don't apply here.

I just needed to make one quick stop to pick up a bouquet of flowers and then drive directly to the airport to collect my client. Nearing the entrance, I turned on my signal and eased into the far right lane. Upon entering the parking area, I hesitated for only a second, applied my brakes lightly, making sure I was turning into the right place. Then at that exact moment, halfway into the driveway, I heard the sickening noise of squealing tires, crunching metal and breaking glass.

Time seemed to stop as my car spun around to face oncoming traffic. It settled, with half of it in the driveway of the mall and half of it in the street.

What just happened? Surreal, I was afraid to move. *Was I okay? How about the car?*

As I sat there, assessing my areas of pain, I breathed deeply, trying to calm the thousands of thoughts flying through my head.

As my mind refocused, I saw what had hit me–a Mexican taxi van, known as a *colectivo*–also known for crazy driving. I knew to avoid them at all costs! Filled to its' maximum capacity with people, it had tried to jet past me on the right. The driver grossly misjudged both the speed and distance he needed to pass me. The bus hit the beautiful beamer on the right rear quarter panel so hard that my car and the bus were now one piece of crunched metal.

The driver, a middle aged man with a hitch in his gait, and a concerned expression, jumped out of his bus and ran to me speaking rapidly in Spanish. *"Esta bien, Senora?"*

I yelled, "No, I'm not okay!" in English—*forgetting* that I was in Mexico. Closing my eyes, I wanted to will this accident away. My head cleared. I realized that *I needed to take charge of the situation or the situation would take charge of me.* Just then, I received another "ding."

"I'm at the airport!" came the text message from my client, Evelyn.

As it got later, the sun's glare was even more severe, matching the intensity of this heated situation. I slowly climbed out of the only door that wasn't jammed by the accident.

In a flicker of sanity, I called Avis, my car rental agency. Soon an independent claims officer arrived, bustling, officious and carrying a very proper looking clipboard as he looked over the melded vehicles. "This is clearly your fault. You need to sign a waver admitting guilt and you will be free to go."

The claim officer's words hit me like a blow to the stomach. Thoughts of doubt flickered. *Was it my fault? Had I turned from the middle lane as the representative suggested?* No, I was sure I hadn't. *Would they believe me? A foreigner with limited Spanish, driving a BMW? Was the system already rigged against me?*

Just then, a man with graying hair appeared—handsome with his closely trimmed beard and intense brown eyes. His self-assured voice spoke, "I saw everything," in flawless English. With absolute authority and confidence he went on to explain how the bus had been tailgating and for some unknown reason, had tried to pass my car on the right as I had started to turn.

"And yes, I'm prepared to make a statement, he said, "These bus drivers are dangerous and they should be held accountable."

I stood there speechless, which isn't a normal state for me. Then, after I let his words sink in, I allowed a few of the tears I had been holding back to escape. I knew he had been sent to me... my guardian angel. Feeling not so alone, maybe there was a ray of light, after all.

Just then, a serious looking policeman approached, speaking rapid fire Spanish. He took control. I couldn't understand a word he was saying. The accident had muddled my brain and my Spanglish. I was in shock!

The claims officer was doing his best to translate, but his English was worse than my Spanglish, except that I did catch this: "You can go to jail or the hospital, you must decide." The policeman was trying to do me a favor by giving me the choice of going to the hospital, even if I didn't fully understand that at the time.

My guardian angel leaned over and whispered to me, "Go to the hospital, jails in Mexico are not pleasant places."

With glazed-over eyes, I looked intently at him and asked, "Are you an angel?" He just smiled.

Zombie-like, I was loaded into the claims officer's car and taken to the gringo hospital. A young nervous doctor checked me over, then, x-rayed my neck. I waited an hour, and then two other doctors arrived to announce that I had an ever so slight neck injury. They insisted I put on a padded neck brace that were so common in the U.S. thirty years ago, and take pain medicine from a dubious looking bottle with no label. I was then installed in a small private room with a policewoman posted just outside my door. I may have been in the hospital, but I was clearly under arrest.

Back to my client Evelyn... I could only text... "Evelyn, I've been placed in custody at a hospital because of a car accident. I won't be able to pick you up. Collect your luggage and walk out to the taxi stand in front of the airport. Give the driver the address of the resort. When you get to the condo, check in and then I will reach out first thing tomorrow morning."

I felt Evelyn might become anxious after learning the unexpected change of plans, but instead she displayed bravery and responded texting, "Pamela, is this your way helping me build my confidence?" along with a smiling emoji.

Poor Evelyn, stuck in a taxi with a 45-minute drive from the airport, alone, in a country she had never visited, with a driver who didn't speak a lick of English. I later learned that Evelyn had serious abandonment issues dating back to her childhood. In fact, what we had planned to address in our "Leaders in Paradise" weekend had to do with facing the things that were holding her back from performing at her peak in life. It had been my goal to surface and work through whatever fears and blocks showed up throughout our weekend. Well… as I sat locked in my hospital/cell room, without question, my police guard was going to see that Evelyn had a head start on that lesson…

By this time, I'm beginning to laugh, because nothing is going as planned–nothing is working. The battery on my phone was nearly dead; my phone charger and computer were still back at the condo. A cloud of anxiety was swirling around me, taxing my strength and resolve. The accident had shaken and disoriented me; my careful planning and controlled schedule evaporated. It was becoming apparent that without intervention I could be trapped in my hospital cell until Monday, as their traffic court had already closed for the weekend.

Suddenly, I thought of my heroine, the "Unsinkable Molly Brown." I felt a little bit like her right now. You know the one, don't you? Officially, she is Margaret Tobin "Molly Brown," who became famous as the heroic survivor of the Titanic shipwreck.

That night as I climbed into my hospital bed, locked in my room all alone, I took a deep breath and closed my eyes. And then, I heard a voice, my voice say, "Pamela, this is what you do. You rise above problems. You can do this!" At that moment, the victim mentality was shut down, and the leader welled up. No way was I going to give in to fear! I was NOT leaving without my adventure in Mexico, I was NOT leaving my client stranded, and I WAS flying home on Monday! I knew exactly what I had to do.

Friday morning, first thing, I called the Avis number and politely insisted that they get me out of there. Two mis-informed representatives showed up midday and painted the picture of me walking right out that door, right now—free! I simply had to sign the waiver stating that the accident was MY fault. If it was not my fault, then it was necessary to stay. I gave them a polite and warm send off *without* me signing the waiver. I believe in having my cake and being able to eat it, too.

The next step was clear—use the hospital phone and call Avis, *again*. Have them summon my appointed attorney to my hospital room/jail cell immediately. Determination and a sense of injustice replaced all fear. I wanted this issue solved, now!

Hours later, a supportive Avis representative arrived along with my appointed attorney, both of them anxious and sweating profusely. Together, we hammered out a plan of how to get me out the hospital. His last comment as he headed out the door: "I'll get back to you when I resolve this."

I responded with, "When will that be?" Having spent a lot of time in Mexico, I knew even the Mexican people laugh about a comment such as this!

By then, it was very late, and even though the tide was turning in my favor, I had to accept that I'd be spending a second night in the hospital. I made arrangements to have my client delivered to my hospital cell, and we had an amazing coaching session—about attracting chaos, abandonment issues, and releasing control.

Once I saw my need to control every outcome instead of allowing life's flow to teach the bigger lesson, I was ready to release this chaos as well; a big chink in my armor was finally identified and mended. We were duo clients.

Shortly after Evelyn left, heading back to the resort, I leaned out to say "Goodnight" to my police guard; she had already dozed off. Best not to wake her.

Next morning, I awoke to rays of bright sunshine, dancing across the room. I was well rested and knew good things were about to happen… Within minutes, a doctor arrived loaning me his iPhone charger to revive my dead phone. Then, a second nurse came in, also smiling and cheerful. She offered me a fourth bottle of water in exchange for practicing her English. I felt like a celebrity, and wondered who else would drop by.

In less than thirty minutes, an exuberant Avis representative phoned to tell me that we had won the case! Another hour later, both the Avis representative and the attorney arrived beaming. They had settled everything! It was ruled that the bus driver had been at fault. Once the police chief signed my release, I would be free to go. Avis would not be charging me anything for the accident. The company also provided me a brand new Ford Fusion, with bells and whistles, and a warning system to help prevent accidents. *Inwardly, I* was grateful. My decision to rent from Avis for all future rentals was sealed.

This was cause for celebration! The two bottles of champagne I salvaged from the wreckage were given to each, and then we all had a big hug fest–so much for the neck brace! I extended my heartfelt thanks for all they had done for me, and thought… I'm outta' here!

Then, the strangest thing happened. While making my way out of the hospital, the nurses, doctors and orderlies all gave me a warm farewell, and asked to be friends on Facebook. My police guard insisted on carrying my things to the car—*okay that was going a bit far, but it makes for a great ending*—in reality she nodded her head politely and rushed to her next job, probably something way more exciting than guarding the door of a woman who didn't even speak her language.

What started as a bizarre accident and incarceration ended up a wonderful opportunity to empower others and myself. *Kindness with confidence became my most effective tool.*

Evelyn and I spent the rest of the VIP weekend exploring underground Cenotes, swimming with sea turtles and zip-lining over a secret lagoon—as well as coaching while basking in the Mexican sun and dining in 4-star restaurants.

On our last evening, my client Evelyn inquired how soon our next adventure could be…

Pamela Cournoyer

Pamela Cournoyer is unique and proven, as an extremely knowledgeable and fun business leadership coach. She integrates her coaching, in a distinctive training adventure called "Leaders in Paradise"—*growing leaders in exotic places. Where she adeptly teaches how to get your own people to follow you anyplace.* In the Paradise of choice, she offers a rip-roaring all inclusive leader adventure and team engagement training combined into one! She helps business and organizational leaders recognize, beyond a shadow of a doubt, that they are a conscious, compelling, incredible and powerful in their leadership style. As a leadership performance coach, she instills and reminds leaders that they are destined to make a huge difference in the world. She brings true clarity of direction for leaders and their team, because all *do not* roll equally. This includes motivational savvy leading to greater profits, unparallelled people shaping abilities, composure during volatile situations and influential communication skills. Pamela is passionate about all aspects of her work, bringing leaders to a place of greater confidence, and belief that they are truly rare and valuable.

pamela@powerfulandtrue.com

www.LeadersInParadise.com

THE JOURNEY OF A THOUSAND MILES BEGINS
BENEATH ONE'S FEET."

—LAO TZU

Coloring Life with a Spirit of Gratitude

JEAN FARISH, PH.D.

A profound dream marked a pivotal moment of grace—and the hand of God upon my life. In this dream, I was in the hospital room of my grandmother, who passed away over a decade ago. And there, in the bathroom, was a shocking sight—my grandmother was lying dead in a tub of water.

I screamed, as I lay on my bed crying from the depths of my heart. My skin felt suffocated from my clothing—drenched with water. Immediately, I felt a presence lift the heavy wet blanket of clothing from my body. I discerned, "Lift the cloak of heaviness…" and "Come to me all who are weary and burdened and I will give you rest." This is a scripture from Matthew 11:28.

Embedded in this dream were clear instructions. "Rise up and shed the cloak of heaviness (personal darkness, struggle, fear, and exhaustion) and replace it with the internal "spiritual garment" of praise—a spirit of gratitude—to drive out the darkness that helps bring victory over life's quagmire of overwhelming circumstances. Clearly, I was told that the spirit of gratitude was the ultimate victory out of the darkness I was in. Even though I counseled others, my spirit was murky, heavy-laden with my own self-critic, feelings of victimization in relationships, and the everyday struggles life had presented me.

Before this dream, I had been well aware that I was in an emotional tailspin, with an unwelcome, uninvited guest at my door—unrelenting and daunting, trying to drag me down into the bog. On the verge of spiritual collapse, the signs and symptoms were apparent with my loss of appetite, sleeplessness, negative thinking, and feelings of utter hopelessness.

I repeatedly focused on my imprudent decisions that made me emotionally vulnerable. Too often, I would seek fulfillment from others with great disillusionment. As I sensed the unrelenting and disrupting knocking from deep within me, I had to fervently acknowledge the old adage, "Counselor heal thyself." I was about to learn valuable lessons in healing and how to overcome adversity.

I couldn't deny it, spiritual depression had taken hold, deep within my soul—a sense of meaninglessness overtook me. This crisis of faith and feelings of abandonment were exacerbated by a series of life events.

The dream became a pivotal experience that enabled me to begin anew, to heal myself—moment-by moment. It began by supplanting negative thoughts with positive ones of love, peace, joy and harmony. Once again, I was able to remember heartwarming experiences that resurrected my spirit. As I began to acknowledge and accept a myriad of feelings that surfaced, it was as if I was a screaming child needing compassion—and God met that need in marvelous and miraculous ways.

"The goal of spiritual practice is full recovery, and the only thing you need to recover from is a fractured sense of self."

—MARIANNE WILLIAMSON

Healing my sense of self...

My close friend helped me process the dream—spiritually. I sensed that the hospital represented my need for healing. The corpse, that was my grandmother, was actually me. I had drowned from the overwhelming grief of my burned-out, stressed-out emotional state which represented a critical and core aspect of myself that had died.

My desperate crying represented my repressed sadness that was being purged and released for purification. I felt death was a metaphor for underlying need for transformation, major life change and rebirth, transitioning from the old to the new. This dream prompted me to surrender, and witness the proof of God's care. Rebirth and renewal began to emerge as I was able to 'let go' of the tests of faith in my life, and much of the loss and sadness I had experienced.

Loss—*that tangible feeling of sadness that overtakes us* when we have to live without someone we need and love— or the loss we feel when we lose (or can't achieve) the material things that we succumb to believing define us—was at the center of all my dark depression and pain.

Looking back on it, the "straw that broke the camel's back," was a material thing. I lost my car, and that particular *loss* seemed to excavate the very cornerstone of my being, which led to the tumbling down of my whole self, brick by brick, each laid on an already shaky foundation.

My raw emotions were rapidly exposed with the undercurrent of faulty beliefs that were weaved through significant life events. They all had become too much to carry and bear!

Interestingly, the loss of my car triggered this unresolved grief that was caving in on me—from the pile upon pile of difficult life events: loss in relationships; betrayal of friendships and people close to me; the loss of my safe and sacred space in Hurricane Katrina (little condo), and other cherished material possessions—*lost*.

I had loss through the deaths of endearing people in my life—including my grandmother, my first boyfriend in high school was killed in a car accident; my colleague and business partner was killed in a car accident; and my mentor in my doctoral program was killed in a fatal airplane crash. After each of these important losses, I did what lots of people do—I just got on with the demands of life, not allowing myself time to grieve.

Two significant thoughts from scripture kept coming to my heart: "Be ye transformed by the renewal of your mind" and "In all thy ways acknowledge him and he shall direct your path."

My pending transformation renewed my daily choices and my thought patterns. I took notice of inspiring thoughts, seeking to understand their significance in living my own life. And people appeared, as if angels. One can never know, but in my heart there seems to be no other explanation.

It can only be called a strange occurrence: an old man mysteriously appeared when I had car trouble. He transported my car, and remained in contact with me during a time of great life distress and transition. He remained in contact with me until all was well in my life—then disappeared, never to be heard from again.

Deep reflections became common, which brought life

change and personal accountability, such as, "How am I treating myself in this moment? Am I receiving answers? What valuable lessons must I learn? What hidden gifts are embedded in this experience?"

Being the gatekeeper of my thoughts, and alert to the inner critic, required me to be present moment-by-moment. Supplanting negative thoughts with positive ones of love, peace, joy and harmony, and remembering heart opening experiences resurrected my spirit.

And as I became attentive to a myriad of feelings that surfaced within me, it was as if I was a screaming child who needed attention and compassion. I did!

Becoming the nurturer of my own heart was healing. Meditation and silence helped me gain clarity and ease. I sought divine guidance for my next steps. Visualizing a clear picture of my desires and positive outcomes, was paramount to transcending this compounded grief that had weighed me down.

In my journal, I wrote about what I was "grateful" for—and I began to keep a gratitude bowl visible, jotting down thoughts of gratitude. The bowl remains on my desk to this day. The spirit of gratitude was the ultimate victory out of the darkness, heaviness, victimization and struggle.

Recognizing how much I had been grappling in this disillusionment and darkness, I realized I had been "dead" to myself. My feelings and needs ignored, due to the compounded grief from loss, and my lack of self-worth.

It was a process, but gratitude for the tremendous *color* in life emerged. I began to watch for and expect good things. The car that represented the catalyst for grieving all losses was mysteriously replaced.

Seeing an ad with a picture of a car, the car of my dream

that I had visualized, I called immediately. A very sweet lady answered; I explained my predicament—I wanted it. She said, "I have a number of buyers interested, but I want you to have it." She significantly reduced the price.

When *she knocked* on my door, I opened it to see a very sweet, soft spoken lady.

Was she an angel? Her name was Miriam, and translated in Hebrew means "raises up, elevates, brings up." We remained in contact almost daily, before the purchase, with her reinforcing her joy for me to have the car, and immediately after, too. She wanted to ensure my satisfaction. As time passed, I was unable to reach her. However, embedded in the car were, and still are, musical tracks of uplifting spiritual songs with messages of faith, praise and victory.

I tell this story to touch your life, and to help you see that a challenge can prove to be an invitation to "wake up." And in doing so, heal the broken heart, open the dormant, closed heart—and ultimately overcome adversity. Loss, of all types, is a universal experience, yet a very private one—which can take any one of us on a journey of transformation, as we rebuild, renew and reconnect with our inner self. In doing so, I learned, and you can too, that *we are inseparable from God's love and care.*

Look For The Color In Life

You are "a divine being; a complete and whole" person, but not until judgment, critical thinking and self-doubt are "let go." We don't even try to climb the mountain where rainbows of color reside until we get unstuck below. Relief comes when we realize that we can only climb that mountain by digging deep inside ourselves, and choose to rely on God's grace and mercy. He can do in us, what we cannot do alone—helping us climb up that hard mountain, step-by-step.

Finding Color In Life

Let me share the lessons learned:

Surrender: Surrender becomes necessary when we feel powerless, fragile and broken.

Humility: A spirit of humility keeps us aware of our human limitations. It provides us the capacity to make mistakes without being emotionally devastated. The death of the ego is necessary, because over time false values, beliefs, and attachments imbed. Feelings of self-worth and self-importance over certain things are magnified for all of us in our culture.

Compassion: To avoid self-condemnation, we must learn to forgive and be gentle with ourselves in our broken-ness or mistakes. A compassionate spirit enables us to confront unresolved losses that compound current losses. We must properly grieve all types of loss, to promote healing.

Resilience: The ability to bounce back from life's difficulties—it is adopting flexibility and hardiness in our lives, as we commit to learning the lessons well. A resolve to come back stronger is the capstone of recovery.

As much as the loss of anything or anyone we value pains and strains us, sharing our life lessons helps propel each one of us towards greater good and gratitude for what we *do have* in life. This brings a sense of awe that increases the beauty and *color* we see in all areas as we travel along our life's journey.

As for me, I am a work in progress. "I have reclaimed myself." "I am an overcomer." "I am a divine being." "I am whole."

I am learning and perfecting my spiritual practice. By helping others, I help myself. Accept your invitation to "wake up." Look for the sun... the color... the light.

Jean Farish, Ph.D.

Jean Farish, Ph.D., has served as a university administrator, professor, and rehabilitation counselor. As a Life Care Coach and self-help author, her six month tenure in Malaysia was a pivotal juncture of her transformational journey. Immersion in an Oriental culture awakened her to the true essence of life and divine love—creative talents expanded as she volunteered and traveled to remote villages and indigenous communities. Driven by her mission of service, she uses her skills and talents to make a difference in the lives of people through personal development and community enrichment classes. Jean knows that life challenges with valuable lessons continue to inspire her own transformational journey, as she helps others become more insightful and introspective. Her deepest desire is to serve humanity in both grand and simple ways—on a higher spiritual level. She is the founder of Life Care Wellness PEP (Personal Enhancement Project) For Angels for children hospitalized with cancer. "I am the seasoned traveler of the labyrinth. Losing my way and finding my way. Traveling on the beaten path and the road less traveled, eventually finding my way home to the place of spiritual rest and fulfillment." —Dr. Jean Farish

Please visit her website featuring her Loss and Recovery Model (LRM).

www.jeanfarishjourney.com

farishjean@gmail.com

"Difficulties come when you don't pay attention to life's whisper. Life always whispers to you first, but if you ignore the whisper, sooner or later you'll get a scream."

—Oprah Winfrey

Do You Hear The Whisper?

RHONDA CULVER

I knelt in the church pew, a small seven-year-old snaggle-tooth, chocolate girl with two pony tails and a part down the middle of my head. I wore the typical white collared button-down shirt and a dark forest green skirt (my school uniform). I was attending the typical mass which was required by the grammar school that I attended, but something was different for me today, from other days in church. As I knelt, I breathed in and felt a warmth all over. A warm, comfortable and familiar sensation was especially noticeable in my heart space—leaving me peaceful and secure. I could almost see it—I envisioned a moon-colored glowing light emanating around my chest area... making me feel *oh so comfortable*. I knew whenever I felt this; I was not alone, that there was something or someone so much more powerful and loving, the Divine, my Heavenly Father, God, with me.

I didn't know it at the time, nor did I hear anything. I felt it though—a whisper from my soul. My soul whisper was not in words, but a sensation that gave me heartfelt meaning: *You are safe, you are loved, you are not alone.* I felt it intuitively, although at that time I hadn't a clue what intuitive meant.

My friend, the soul, does whisper. Have you heard your soul whisper in the past? Do you hear the whisper now? Have you ever received guidance and hunches, often from something that is difficult to explain? The whispers of our soul provide us with inner wisdom; often they are clues that will lead us to our purpose in life. Many times they are gently guiding us towards work or endeavors that will make our heart sing. The messages whispered are often recurring, to get our attention and remind us of what would make us happy. When we are busy with the hustle and bustle of life, it is often very difficult to hear the whispers.

Well, as for me the elementary school years rolled on and as they did, my love for reading, and especially my love for writing became evident. When I wrote, I felt that warm sensation that I felt in mass—and again time seemed to stand still. I wrote compositions, I wrote poems, I recited poems. I even appeared a few times on a local television show geared toward African Americans called "Get It On." My soul seemed to whisper, although very softly, "Girlfriend, you love to write, you were meant to write, so you should write…"

But honestly, I don't think I was listening. I just wrote, because I loved doing it. I was the only child in my family for nine years. I often felt alone and sometimes even lonely. *I was not alone, but I forgot.* This happened when I was too busy, and *did not* hear the whispers.

Life went on, and high school years brought fun, friends and some social events—and more importantly, it brought about the need to make a decision on a college major and a career direction. I knew I loved to write, but what would I do with this love? After speaking with school counselors and family members, I chose to major in 'business' an area that appeared to have more salary stability, versus a focus on 'writing' and creating. I stopped spending time writing—the activity I loved that made time stand still… and helped me to hear.

Yes, college was fun from a social standpoint. The coursework was just that 'work', not much creativity, not fun at all, though it was valuable with lots of learning since much of the information was new to me. Certainly writing was a necessity for the major, however, the writing was technical and for me, a bit boring.

After college graduation, I began working in the accounting field, although I did not major in accounting. Accounting had been one of my least favorite courses in school, however, the position fell into my lap and it appeared to be a good career track financially. My focus was on salary… the dollars.

I obtained an MBA (Master's in Business) with an accounting emphasis, and also a CPA certificate (Certified Public Accounting). I had the degrees and certificates; I worked in the field, however, I never loved the field—my heart was somewhere else. I had chosen, no doubt, to move away from my love of writing. I believe that burning desire for something propels one to go deeply into their area of passion. And since I had no passion for accounting, I delved only to the adequate level that was required for the task or positions that I held.

Recognizing that I had moved away from what made my heart sing, the whispers began speaking to me again—and they became louder and more frequent. They began befriending me. I took notice! The whisper warned me when I was going to have a car accident; it sometimes predicted events; it warned me when certain romantic relationships were not in my best interest; it warned me when someone was being untrue towards me, and more importantly, it gave me ideas of products that I could create and write about.

I had no clue how I could create and write what the whispers were revealing to me. I did not have the knowledge or confidence required to pull these softly spoken suggestions all together, so I ignored them. The whisper always worked in my best interest, but I didn't understand. It frightened me, and I asked and prayed to God that it stop.

No longer feeling the warm, comfortable and familiar sensation I felt as a child, the whispers stopped after I prayed for them to go away. I continued in the corporate world and began obtaining positions with increasing responsibility. However, I knew in my heart that I belonged somewhere else, I knew that I should be creating and writing. I knew it deeply; however, I did not know what to do with that knowing. How would I get from where I was to where my heart wanted to be? From a financial perspective, I was comfortable.

After many years in the corporate world, I still felt discontent. Outward success didn't quiet my soul that felt it was supposed to be doing something else.

I had known that I wanted to make a leap from the corporate world for quite some time. One year, 2006 to be exact, I made the decision to do so and I jumped without knowing where I would land. I was on my own. Just like that. What a wonderful feeling, at first. After all, I had three to five years of reserves to pay my living expenses, and I had a healthy retirement... or so I thought.

If I had to do it all over again, and when I'm coaching someone else, I advise, "Get your living expenses as low as you can, and also conservatively do your best to ensure that you have income coming in to cover those expenses." Because when I made the leap, I had several rental properties that 'just about' cash flowed ($100 per month or less, negative cash flow). I also had made a moderate income in remodeling residential real estate—a field that was fairly new to me at the time.

It should come to no surprise that when the economy declined and the bubble peaked in 2008, the rental rates plummeted, and my rental properties, with a small negative cash flow were the source of sizeable *cash leaks.* The full gut remodels in my pipeline, became a cash drain. After a few poor decisions to try to remain afloat, I lost all of my financial wealth—*just like that!*

What a stressful experience, to say the least. Disappointment and disenchantment took its toll on my psyche and self-esteem. What now?

After the real estate bubble burst, I obtained a real estate license and worked with several brokerages, two of which I was either part-owner or owner. Initially, my earnings ranged from 15-25 percent of my previous corporate salary. I obtained government healthcare and food stamps just to remain afloat. I was amazed that I was able to survive on that income level, but I made it somehow.

I assisted and watched as many savvy investors picked up fantastic and unbelievable real estate deals. Previously I could have paid cash for many of these deals, but my 'financial' well was dry. This period brought on a wealth of information and learning for me: starting businesses, terminating businesses, analyzing real estate investments, learning the marketing and sales cycle, managing cash on an extremely slim budget, just to name a few. I earned a Ph.D. in *what to do*, and what *not* to do, especially in real estate, business, and with one's cash. However, as much as I previously loved owning real estate, and as much as I liked working with others in their acquisition and sale of real estate, I still felt discontent and inner unrest.

One day, a friend introduced me to a lady, who I believe was an earth angel to give me a message. This was not an unusual occurrence for me. I have periodically had unknown people stop and provide me with messages. The lady told me that I had a gift and that I had taken it and stuffed it in a box and put it away. I instantly knew she was referring to the whispers, my *intuition*.

I had asked it to stop because it frightened me. If I look back and reflect, however, the whispers did nothing but guide and protect me. The lady also told me that there was something I should be doing, and that the Divine would be there to guide me and help me—that I was not alone.

How could I forget that? I AM NOT ALONE. I knew what she meant immediately. I knew what I should be doing, and it was creating and writing.

Out of the ashes the Phoenix rises! I am finally listening to the whispers of my soul to write and create. And it is absolutely perfect and divine that this is occurring after thirty years of experience in the corporate world; it enables me to write and create product copy around personal finance and real estate (do's and don'ts)—to provide trusted help to those in need of guidance with their finances.

It is perfectly fine, that instead of going from Point A to Point B (to move into writing straight from college), that I am going from A (college) to C (accounting and finance), to D (real estate), and then back to B (writing). I have extensive business and leadership experience, which offers valuable, helpful information to the targeted audience of people to which I write. I am finally honoring and trusting my soul whisper, and it brings me so much excitement and joy.

Now, what about you? Do you hear the whisper? Have you heard the whisper in the past? Do you ignore and suppress the whisper? Or do you honor and trust the guidance from your inner self, your soul?

Stop. Listen. Act.

Rhonda Culver

Rhonda Culver is a personal finance expert and author. After exiting from her corporate career in 2006, she established a career in real estate investments. At that time, she had a net worth of close to $2M. After the economy crashed, along with a few poor choices, Rhonda lost it all and filed bankruptcy. Turning her financial condition around equipped her with many lessons learned, and the knowledge and desire to help and teach others how to improve their finances. Now the founder of two thriving companies, she credits her turnaround to finally listening to the whispers of her soul. She knows God is guiding her life and her optimistic attitude.

She has recently completed the creation of her online course, "Transform Your Finances NOW!" Rhonda's passion is teaching, speaking and guiding others in how to improve their personal finances.

Rhonda, a CPA, also holds a BS and a MBA from Arizona State University and is an adjunct accounting professor in the Maricopa Community College system. Rhonda, previously a finance executive at American Express, spent over thirty years in industry accounting.

rculver3@msn.com

www.transformyourfinancesnow.com

"To desert the Truth in the hour of need is to prove that we do not know the Truth... The person who can throw himself with a complete abandon into that Limitless Sea of Receptivity, having cut loose from all apparent moorings, is the one who will always receive the greatest reward."

— Ernest Holmes, *The Science of Mind*

Get In, Sit Down, Shut Up, And Hold On!

LINDA FINLEY

The job interview was Friday, April 2, after work, and I was eager to go. A year before, I had completed four years of training and testing to receive the license and title of "Minister." My administrative work at the large radio broadcasting company where I currently worked was my version of an actor working as a waitress while waiting for "the big break." (At that time, rules in our denomination set a cap on the number of staff ministers in each location, and the Center I attended had reached that limit, so I was not able to activate my minister's license locally.)

I had known Debra, the Sales Manager at the mall where I was about to interview, for some time. She had been a sales rep at the radio station before taking the job at the mall.

My job at the station was serving as administrator for both the general manager and the sales department. Debra appreciated my work and really wanted me as her assistant. If I went to work there, I would trade my twenty miles a day round trip commute to a two block round trip walk from my apartment—at least while I was still in the role of "working as a waitress waiting for the big break."

When I got there, I met with Debra, the business manager and the general manager. It was a wonderful experience, with each of them praising my resumé, my skill set, my demeanor in the interview. Part of my work history included twelve years of owning my own business, so I had strong management, bookkeeping and personnel experience, in addition to clerical and graphic art skills.

By the end of two hours together, I learned the general manager planned to retire in a year and the business manager was being groomed to take over his position. They needed to check with corporate headquarters, but they made me an offer to come on board as Debra's assistant, and also train to take over the role of business manager at the end of the first year.

It was a much bigger job than I had expected, and I was over-the-moon happy. It would be two to three weeks before they would have a definitive answer from the home office, and they were confident it would be "a go."

As I drove to my favorite tavern for a beer, hoping my friends would still be there waiting to hear about my interview, I realized something even bigger was going on inside me.

If I was that good here, I was that good anywhere! Two hours of positive, affirming input from three people in positions of power were pretty convincing... I was a plum!

I told my buddy, Bill, that this was the encouraging push I needed to leave everything behind and make the move to the San Francisco Bay Area in California. I had wanted to go there for a few years, and now it seemed within the realm of possibility.

My dream was to start a ministry work of my own. It

seemed now might very well be the time to do so!

That night I got out a map of the Bay Area and a list of our denomination's centers there. I made marks on the map wherever there were existing centers, because I wanted to establish a center of my own in a place there was none. There were three towns, Novato (in Marin County), Petaluma and Sonoma (in Sonoma County) where there were no centers of our denomination.

I did a web search of the three communities, and fell in love with Petaluma—it seemed like just what I had been seeking. I drafted an email to the Home Office of our denomination and put in a request to start a new work in Petaluma, even though I had never been there, nor did I know a soul there.

Because I needed to have a steady income while I got my new work started, I then did a search for employment agencies in online newspapers. I sent in a few resumés by email, and figured I had a pretty productive Friday evening!

Monday morning, I got an email from an agency in Larkspur, in Marin County, asking me to please come in for an introductory appointment. I did some research on the bus system, booked an Amtrak round trip ticket and called in sick on Wednesday, taking the 6:00 a.m. train to Richmond, catching BART (San Francisco Bay Area Rapid Transit), combined with bus travel, to finally wind up in Larkspur, making it to my appointment by 11:00 a.m.

The whole process was a bit nerve-shattering, not knowing where I was going, what to expect, or how the area looked. I just trusted that it would all work out—and it did.

The people at the agency could not believe what I had gone through to get there. They administered tests of my math, spelling and typing skills, which the owner said were some of the best they had seen. (Example: p. or pp. for pages, rather than pg. was apparently not known by many others.)

In addition, they liked my interview, and so they sent me to the next building to interview for an administrative position with a leadership training company.

The firm I was interviewing with had high ethical standards, and appealed to my sense of doing "good work." Lastly, the people at the agency helped me make my train connection, and I arrived safely home Wednesday night near midnight.

Over the next three weeks, I had several by-phone and in-person interviews with various people in the company, and was told that everyone who had connected with me really wanted to hire me. At the same time, the owner of the employment agency said that with my skills, she could keep me busy until I found a full time job if for some reason the potential job fell through.

I turned in my notice at my current job, let the people at the mall know I would be unable to accept their generous offer, and made plans to move to Petaluma.

After another train trip and the help of someone I met online (another story, for another time), I spent Saturday in Petaluma, looking for rooms to rent. I spent four hours either calling numbers where no one answered, or getting through only to see rooms that just did not feel right. And then I had the chance to view one last spot before I needed to catch my train home. The room was upstairs, with all kinds of built-ins and a huge closet, plus a sitting room shared with the person in the other rented room.

After filling out applications all day, I asked the woman if I could fill out an application, and she said, "No." She did not want an application; she wanted to rent to me. She was familiar with Science of Mind, and loved the fact that I was moving there to start a new work in this philosophy of spiritual living.

I opened my checkbook to write out a deposit check, only to discover I was out of checks. Incredibly, she entrusted me with one of her deposit slips, and told me to put the money in her bank account, via electronic transfer when I got back to Visalia!

So… I headed home to Visalia Saturday night and went to church on Sunday, where I shared with my community that I was moving the following week and needed to borrow some money to make things go a bit smoother. With moving expenses, I was going to be on a very tight budget the first couple of months. I wondered if they wanted to get rid of me, because people were standing in line to write out checks for me. Amazingly, I got double the amount I had asked for, and most of it was gifted to me.

Monday, I got a call from the employer in Larkspur, telling me they would have a decision on Friday, but everything looked good. I set about the business of packing and getting things I could not take with me into storage. I wrapped up my work at my current job, where I would finish on Friday, before leaving on Saturday for Petaluma.

Thursday evening, I got a call from the company in Larkspur. A former employee of the company had moved back to the area and contacted them to see if there was any work available. I was told that, as much as they liked me, I was an unknown quantity and she was a "sure thing."

So… here I was in an uncertain transition. My job ending in the morning, my apartment nearly packed up, I had to trust that the agency would find me work.

I called the agency Friday morning, and they had just

gotten an order for an almost identical position to the one I had been interviewing for, and it was in Novato, twenty miles closer to Petaluma. Could I interview on Tuesday? I could.

My friends, Sandra and Ed, loaded my belongings in a U-Haul van; I got my car loaded, and off to Petaluma we drove. I got my stuff moved in—after discovering my beloved bookcases would not fit up the circular wrought iron stairs that led to my room. Well, so it was, and there I was, starting a whole new phase of my life.

I went to the job interview on Tuesday, and on Thursday was hired to start the following Monday.

All this took place between April 2 and May 20. It was a whirlwind experience, and I came to understand the phrase I had seen on license plate frames—"Get in, sit down, shut up, and hold on…" described how my life felt for those weeks.

I had an intention to move to the San Francisco Bay Area and start a work, which grew out of that interview on April 2. The request I filed to start a work in Petaluma was approved. So everything conspired for things to fall into place in ways I could never have planned.

The employment agency that pulled a rabbit out of its hat the first day I arrived, and the day that job fell through? Its business name was "Perfect Timing." And the room that I found at the last minute was in a big Victorian house at the corner of Pleasant and Prospect. The company that hired me after I moved there decided three months later to find a property in Petaluma. They moved there, so my commute went from ten miles to two. In a way, I was still an "actor working as a waitress," to earn a living; and I had begun a permanent "gig" at my own center!

So, in forty-nine days, I went from seeking a new job in a town where I had lived for thirty years, to starting a whole new chapter in my life—a new beginning. Of course, I had to be ready and willing, and I had to hear and believe the comments of the people who interviewed me there at the mall. And I had to be willing to let those words awaken me to whom I could really become, and then act on them.

Is life sending you messages? Are you hearing the words, the comments, the ideas that may be guiding you to take your next step? I remember one time hearing that opportunity does not just knock once—it is knocking twenty-four hours a day, seven days a week and we are simply "too busy" to notice.

Sit up! Listen! Notice! And then be prepared for a ride...

Linda Finley

Linda Finley: "I stand for a world where inclusion and collaboration lead us to embody a reverence for all life." For the past twenty-three years of Linda's life she has been teaching a philosophy known as the "Science of Mind." It is part of the American family of denominations known as New Thought; the organization's locations are called Centers for Spiritual Living. Linda has been a minister in this faith since 1999, serving communities in Petaluma, CA and Eugene, OR. This teaching emphasizes personal empowerment, while discovering and living out individual gifts, of which Linda realizes she has been working at all of her life. Whether it was her time spent working as an eligibility worker in the Tulare County Welfare Department in the 1970s, or as an employment counselor in private agencies during the late 1970s and early 1980s, she has used her gifts and skills—and this includes work managing a wholesale hardware outlet for contractors and cabinet makers, and the years, 1984 to 1996, when she owned the Lucky Penny Pub. In all regards, her life's work has been to connect people with their gifts, and then with jobs and people that supported them in their growth.

www.csleugene.org

www.facebook.com/revlindaf

"...NOTHING IS AS UNCOMFORTABLE, DANGEROUS AND HURTFUL AS BELIEVING THAT I'M STANDING ON THE OUTSIDE OF MY LIFE LOOKING IN AND WONDER-ING WHAT IT WOULD BE LIKE IF I HAD THE COURAGE TO SHOW UP AND LET MYSELF BE SEEN."

—BRENÉ BROWN, *DARING GREATLY*

Learning to Live an Authentic Life: A Mother's Gift

MERI JUSTIS

When will I be able to fall apart and cry until there are no more tears? When will I be able to be the weak, messy and emotional one? When can I let go of being the responsible one and honor my own feelings; be real and authentic?

I grew up in a big family with lots of kids, and I am smack dab in the middle of my seven siblings. I am the youngest of the older kids and the oldest of the younger ones, and not really a part of either group. Born in the 50s in a time and in a neighborhood where having lots of kids and chaos was the norm.

Our days were filled with simple, healthy and fun activities—riding bikes, swimming in the neighbor's pool and playing baseball in the middle of the street. More often than not our house was filled with raucous activity, out of control laughter and lots of yelling and screaming. And most of the time it was too much for me.

Somewhere in my childhood amidst all the messiness and noise I took on the role of the responsible kid—if something was wrong, I had an innate sense it was my job to make it better.

At a very young age, I formed a strong bond with my mother, and I loved her with all my heart. I never wanted to be away from her. I never wanted to disappoint her. It was agony for me to see her hurt or angry or upset—and with eight kids that happened a lot.

By nature, I was organized and a hard worker. I would go to great lengths to avoid making mistakes or being wrong. I was a good student; I felt by *being* good, no one could get mad at me. I behaved at home and always did what I was told so I wouldn't get in trouble. I felt this would assure my mother's love and approval.

When I was three, just before the birth of my mother's sixth child, my parents, due to an ultimatum from my mother to my father, joined AA—and our lives were changed for the good—at least for a while.

The next ten years were happy ones, fairly organized and structured, loving and prosperous. Shortly after joining AA my parents began attending a new thought church where we learned that God or Infinite Intelligence dwells within each person, that all people are spiritual beings; and that the highest spiritual principle is to love one another unconditionally. The church also believed that through our thoughts we created our experience. Positive or good thoughts would create a good experience; negative or bad thoughts would create bad experiences. I began to believe that whatever was happening in my life, good or bad was due to my thinking, in other words, it was all and always my fault.

Can you imagine the impact of this on a little eight year old girl—me—who already believed I was responsible for keeping everything peaceful and happy in my family? At this point weak, messy and emotional went on my taboo list. Negativity was avoided at all costs; I gravitated toward all things good. "Stand guardian to the portholes of your mind," from Ralph Waldo Emerson became my mantra, along with "Change your thinking, change your life," a quote from Ernest Holmes. Be strong and responsible and all will be well.

So it began—living my life from the belief that *I could and should control the world* with my thoughts and prayers, and by being a perfectly well behaved child, little Miss Sunshine—and later, demanding the same high expectations of myself as an adult. This left no room for messy, weak or emotional—strong and responsible were the tools I used to navigate through life.

Growing up I had an extraordinary relationship with my mother. I remember sharing many quiet moments and heartwarming conversations with her from early in my childhood, and way into my adult years. As a child, I thought she was beautiful, perfect and incredibly wise. I thought I had the best mom in the neighborhood.

Tragedy struck when I was fourteen and my father left us, leaving five children at home for my mother to raise by herself. She was heartsick and emotionally devastated. I immediately felt the need to hold it all together for us and for her. I was scared to death something bad would happen. I went into "perfectly well behaved, responsible and strong child" mode, fearful she would completely fall apart and even more afraid we would be taken away from her.

This began the way in which I lived my life for the next thirty or so years; holding on to good thoughts, doing the right and responsible thing, navigating away from anything negative or painful. Protecting myself by doing everything a smart, responsible, loving daughter, wife, mother, sister, employee *should do*. The need to be good and steer clear of anything bad was immense. As was the belief that if anything did go wrong, I had caused it with my thinking. A flat tire, a cold, a sick child, a broken appliance, all created by my thinking and my good or bad behavior.

My mother was an incredibly free spirit, yet I felt responsible to take care of her. She was always gracious and grateful for my love and help, but she was also an independent, vibrant and vitally alive woman. She took risks that scared me to death. Once, when I was in my teens, she brought home six French sailors for dinner that didn't speak English. *Who does that?* She thought it would be a good and fun experience for us kids. Six strange, foreign men in the house was not my idea of fun or safe!

Shortly after I graduated from high school, she moved to Hawaii with my three younger siblings to take a half-baked job offer that didn't pan out. She loved the ocean and warm weather and she somehow figured out how making a living in Honolulu with three school age children could work financially. Crazy! She often worked three jobs to make ends meet.

At sixty-three she joined the Peace Corp and went to the Philippines for two-and-one-half years followed by a solo trip around Asia and Europe. Once, while in China, she called me collect to tell me she had met a man thirty years her junior and he wanted to come back to the states with her. Crazy! He didn't, but another one of her "scare me to death" moments. I sometimes felt like I was the responsible mother and she was the daughter.

Her name was Roselyn, she was a lovely woman; smart and fun and full of life. She was an artist. She loved unconditionally. She accepted people where they were and for who they were. She believed with all her heart that every human being was worthy of love and acceptance. Clearly, she wasn't the most responsible person on the planet. A trip to the beach would trump a day at home being responsible cleaning house or doing laundry. The last of the food money for the month might be spent on a picnic lunch instead of milk and bread and peanut butter for the week. People loved her and I adored her. My biggest fear my entire life was losing her, even though she frustrated and scared the heck out of me with her irresponsible antics. I cherished how her loving touch and tender eyes could soothe and comfort me in trying times.

Her death was the most difficult thing I have ever experienced. And I so wish I would have done it differently. Always the strong one, I took on all the doing that needed to be done when we found out she had cancer. I never allowed myself to cry in her arms, or tell her how scared I was to lose her. I *never* let my fear surface. I never fell apart or cried myself to sleep, or even let anyone how hard it was for me.

Instead, I made sure her house was clean, got her papers in order, took care of all her finances, and kept her meds in order. Along with hospice assistance, I saw to it that she had someone with her as much as possible. During that whole three-and-one-half months as she was dying, I never got a chance, *never took the chance,* to breathe in her loving touch and her tender, soothing words; I kept myself busy avoiding the dark side of life—and her death.

Good things happen from hard, seemingly bad things. After her death, weak and messy and emotional took over; for the first time in my life I lost control of myself in grief and sadness. The tears and pain would show up whenever they wanted; I couldn't control it. Soon I realized I didn't want to. It was as if her death gave me permission to fall apart and experience authentic, real, raw emotions. I fell into the deep, dark black hole of pain and loss—and stayed there. I fully embraced it, without any fear of the repercussions that I once believed would come from succumbing to my negative emotions. I somehow knew these powerful, dark emotions were part of authentic living.

I soon realized the worst thing that could ever happen to me had happened; the darkest, scariest thing ever for me was to lose my mother, my Roselyn, my beautiful, loving mother. It happened and I was still here, still functioning, still living my life surrounded by a loving family, caring, supportive friends, doing work that I loved… helping others learn to accept themselves unconditionally—the good, the bad and the ugly.

The funny thing is that prior to her death, I had spent the last several years in a profession where I worked with individuals helping them to expand their awareness to embrace their wholeness—to see that with all their foibles and fears they were still whole and complete.

Now it was my turn. Really? Yes.

My journey began by coming to know my shadow side; the parts of me that I deemed not pretty or worthy of my attention.

I've discovered the essence of life is to live as authentically as we can. And to live authentically means to accept the wholeness of who we are—including our fears and flaws and suffering, all parts of us—the good, the bad and the embarrassing! This means being willing to be present to whatever is arising in the moment; to not avoid, but to feel the fear, the pain, the joy, the suffering without judgment, but with curiosity and acceptance. We are not fully living if we are hiding, avoiding or denying parts of our self.

It is incredibly wonderful to let go of being the strong, stoic responsible one. I am able to allow the weakest parts of me to surface, to really look at them and accept them as part of who I am. I survived my mother's death by learning to accept all of me unconditionally, just the way she did me.

The Spark: Living my own life, being present with myself and my experience—all of it.

It's beautiful to see that my life, just the way it is, good and bad—is whole, perfect and complete.

Meri Justis

Meri Justis has more than twenty-five years in corporate leadership and management, and has expanded her work to include a coaching practice centered on personal development. It emphasizes authenticity—something many leave behind to accommodate the pressures of relationships, expected roles, and careers.

"Discover Your Authentic Life," renews a relationship with one's self—peels back the layers, to help identify and accept all that is whole, perfect and complete. With her unique blend of business experience, and commitment to ongoing personal development, Meri Justis assists clients to generate new thinking and behaviors, to ultimately create the change they desire.

Integrating compassion and insight, Meri provides the tools necessary for her client's personal and organizational success. As a progressive thought leader, she understands the issues of today's complex environment and she works closely with clients to identify and create successful solutions for a variety of challenges.

Meri is a certified "Integral Coach," and has a master's degree in human resources. Corporate leadership has inspired her success as a business consultant, coach and trainer.

Meri's sincerity and professionalism flow naturally when she says, "I love this work because it allows me to do what I most care about—creating and holding the space that allows others to access and live from their own wisdom. I love helping people step into their full, magnificent selves."

Meri@justisgroup.com

"To venture causes anxiety, but not to venture is to lose one's self..."

— Søren Kierkegaard

A Big Move: Embracing The New

MELINDA KAPOR

Adventure can be defined as an activity involving uncertainty, excitement and the unknown. What people find to be exhilarating is as varied as the people themselves. When Helen Keller said *"Life is either a daring adventure or nothing,"* she spoke from profound experience. Rendered deaf, blind and dumb as a very young child, everything that a non-impaired person found mundane became a great adventure for Helen. I wrote her quote in my teenage journal, having no idea where her words would eventually lead me.

A decade later, I arrived in Rome alone, not knowing where I was going, no job and not speaking the language. It was the early 1980s and Ronald Reagan was president. I had nothing guiding me but the resolve to live in Europe, not as a tourist but as a resident. This life-changing adventure was a very big move.

Everyone's life is constantly filled with decisions to make, but a *big move* is when one gets to a "Y" in the road of their life journey and a major choice on which way to go presents itself. One choice is more comfortable than the other; it is known. The other one, a *big move*, pushes the individual outside of his or her comfort zone. These "moves" are not limited to physically relocating; they can be any new experience that is challenging, different from one's norm. All big moves are transformative in perspective and personal growth…if one should so allow.

As the intercultural liaison at an international school in Milan, Italy, my role was to assist newcomers to adjust to the cultural differences of living here. My office became a haven for those that were homesick, missing what was comfortable and familiar. A box of tissues was conveniently located as tears often flowed. Culture shock is a very real and stressful phenomenon, especially when one doesn't speak the host country's language.

Sometimes a woman would arrive in Italy following her spouse for his career opportunity, leaving her own career on hold. This was doubly hard because a sense of purpose, other than family, no longer existed. What I advised is to seize the day…*carpe diem*…and make the most of a new experience that could be incredibly enriching. Instead of staying home, feeding into nostalgia, explore the city, walk the roof of the Duomo, take a day trip. The possibilities were, and are, limitless.

Unfortunately, not everyone took advantage of the time while abroad. Those who had complained the most were also those that cried the hardest when it was time to move back home. Their time had been wasted grumbling instead of embracing the adventure they found themselves in.

> To truly appreciate life, live well in the moment; it will
> never come again.
>
> —Melinda Kapor

My mother instilled in me, early on, a curiosity about other places. She made a *big move* herself when, as a young woman, she left her New England home, traveling west to answer an ad for teachers needed in California. Little did she know, at the start of her two-year contract, that she'd be staying *out West* for thirty-five years.

As a young girl, sitting in an apricot tree, looking over flat fields of the San Joaquin Valley, I dreamt of far-away lands, imagining myself living within the books my mom bought for me. At age five, I had a pen pal in Holland, our mothers writing the letters on our behalf. By the time I was twelve, I had pen pals in countries as varied as Japan, Australia, France, Austria, Italy, India, Brazil, England and Colombia.

For me, going off to college was a *big move*, just northwest an hour and a half from my small hometown. In the 1970s, it wasn't common for college kids to do a year abroad. If it had been, perhaps I would have traveled earlier. I even turned down a trip during my last year of university that my dad offered me to the *Old Country*—the then Yugoslavia. He wanted to show me where his parents had come from. He himself had only been there for the first time a few years before. It greatly moved him to see the origins his family had escaped from, under the heavy influence of the former Ottoman and Austrian Hungarian empires; he wanted me to see it too.

But I wasn't interested. I had a job and a boyfriend and I didn't want to leave either. Thinking back to my young self, I shake my head. If I had said yes, would my dad have booked tickets? I'll never know. It was never discussed again, and I subsequently moved to San Francisco. Less than two years after, my father was diagnosed with leukemia. Five months later he was dead.

He who hesitates often misses his opportunity.
—Chinese proverb

Shortly after my father passed away, his older sister asked me if I would like to join her, her daughter and grandson, on a trip to Yugoslavia. I immediately said yes.

It was my first trip to Europe; Dubrovnik was the first city I'd ever visited outside the United States. Half a world away from California, it was magical. A medieval walled city from the 11th century, it was like stepping back in time. I fell in love with the beautiful Adriatic coast, with the people and the culture. Dubrovnik then, wasn't the tourist destination that it is today. *Stari Grad,* the Old Town, was a living, working city. I appreciated seeing how people were satisfied with less, while taking more time to enjoy family and friends. My ten days there were not enough; I was determined to return.

When I got back to San Francisco, I looked up Yugoslavia in the phone book and found a Yugoslav travel agency. I walked in and got a job. Soon I was managing the office. Nine months after my first trip to Dubrovnik, I went back. It was on this two-week trip that I met someone who would be my catalyst for change.

Back at work in San Francisco and within a few months, I won two free tickets to go anywhere a particular airline flew to, in Europe. I asked my younger brother, Johnny, if he'd like to come with me to Frankfurt, from where we'd continue to Dubrovnik and Herzegovina. He'd been the closest to our father; I knew visiting where our paternal grandparents were from would be as moving an experience for him as it was for me. He readily accepted the invitation. Our time together on that trip became cherished memories, as a year later, Johnny was killed in a tragic accident.

During that third trip to Dubrovnik with my brother, my relationship deepened with a man I'd met on the prior visit. He asked me to meet him in Paris in two months time. "Oh, I can't," was my initial response. But something urged me, "Why not?" I'd already decided to leave San Francisco to go somewhere new. Perhaps his invitation was the spark I needed to try living in Europe. I wanted to grab life, living my own experiences fully rather than reading about somebody else's.

I had no long-term plans, only short-term. I wasn't expecting my relationship to be everlasting; I knew that my boyfriend had to return to Yugoslavia. It was still an Eastern Block country and, as an American, there were no opportunities there for me. France did not draw me, but knowing him would help ease me into a new life overseas. Where to go after Paris? I liked the Mediterranean temperament and the thought of Italy. On one of my last nights in Paris, I heard a voice in a dream that said matter-of-factly: "Go to Rome." And so I did.

After living four years in Rome, I announced to my friends that I was moving to Milan. "But why?", they exclaimed, "You have a life here now." I said it was for work, but really it was due to a *strong feeling* I had… I just knew I had to go. And, as fate would have it, I met my eventual husband the first month in Milan. What I'd perceived to be a work/career path was really the road to my future relationship—an important destination.

We will all have forks in the road during our life journey. I've learned to not rationalize what might be the best or more comfortable way, but to follow the feeling, the inner knowing, and choose wherever it directs me. It's not always that easy; sometimes the decisions are hard. But if I let go and don't over analyze, the answers come. Going to bed at night saying I'll have the answer in the morning helps, as if my subconscious guides me during sleep.

I've also noticed that a check system appears. When the direction is right, things flow into place; when the choice is not the best, all sorts of obstacles appear. Things went smoothly, for example, when I needed to sell my car for extra funds in order to move to Europe. With my ticket already booked for November 1st, I stated that I would sell my car by October 30th. In two weeks of running a newspaper ad, just one person responded. She came to see the car on October 29th, leaving me a deposit and paying me in full on October 30th. I left for Europe right on schedule.

Sometimes people have commented how brave I was to move overseas. Courage is subjective. It's what challenges *you*, not me or anyone else. I don't have the courage to downhill ski; other people do. Deciding on a *big move* has to come from within oneself. Will you regret if you take the easier, more comfortable route? The possibility of regret was something I'd contemplated. I didn't want to arrive at eighty years old, looking back on my life feeling sorry that I hadn't had the daring to make a bold move.

Making a decision to jump into something you've never done before is frightening. However, there is something to be said about facing the fear of the unknown. Perhaps it won't be the right move, but at least you'll never wonder if it was. You'll know for sure—one way or the other. Plus, there is an upside to mistakes and failures in the wealth of knowledge we can glean from them.

A wonderful analogy that I read in a magazine years ago, while waiting in a dentist's office, was found in a fictional story. I wish I could cite the author here, but it's her message and not her name that is remembered. Her character, when faced with a decision, chose not to go with what was safe and sure, what she called *jello*, but opted for the risk… *soufflé*. The soufflé might not turn out, but if it did, it would be memorable and well worth it.

That is what I chose; I opted for the soufflé. I'm grateful for the experiences that have come with it, the people I have met, and the relationships that I've formed for all have far exceeded my greatest imaginings.

Melinda Kapor

An eclectic explorer of life, Melinda Kapor is an intercultural consultant and writer. She enjoys encouraging and inspiring others as they embark upon their own travels, helping them to better understand the obscure feelings that rise up for a particular place that cannot be explained or rationalized. Melinda herself never thought she'd leave her home state, but a first trip to Europe in the early 1980s changed all that. Soon after she was living in Italy, where she still resides today. Besides being a great storyteller in writing and in person, her many interests include amateur photography, some of which she shares at:

www.melindakapor.com

melinda@melindakapor.com

"LIFE IS EITHER A DARING ADVENTURE OR NOTHING."

—HELEN KELLER

It's Time To Go Now...

NATE ROBERTS

woke up in the emergency room at 2:30 a.m. from a dead sleep to the sound of a commanding voice. "It's time to go now…"

"What?" I said.

"It's time to go now," the voice insisted.

"What are you talking about? I've got all these I.V.'s stuck in both arms, stuff strapped and stuck all over my chest. And there's nobody around, so I don't think I'm supposed to be going anywhere right now."

The voice persisted, saying: "They are all busy. A trauma just came in. This isn't rocket science. You know how to unhook that stuff. C'mon, it's time to go!"

Well, if you say so. So… sick or not, I was only twenty-six years old, so up I jumped out of that hospital bed, ripping I.V.'s out of my arms—tearing heart, breathing and blood pressure monitors off my chest— triggering medical alarms all around me.

Needless to say, there was no trauma. *I was the trauma!* I just didn't consciously know that yet. I had finally been admitted to the E.R. that hot desert night just outside the Vegas Strip. I'd just spent five hours heaving; non-stop vomiting—and the only option, the only comfort, seemed to be praying to the porcelain God in our master bedroom.

With no other recourse, I went to the hospital, and joined what might be a typical Las Vegas sight, a dehydrated and sick guy. I sat for two hours in the E.R. waiting area with a bucket ready between my legs while I waited my turn.

However, this E.R. visit wasn't from an *epic* party night out on the town. No, I wasn't that lucky. The card I had drawn in life is that of a Type 1 diabetic. This incident began with a flu bug. And with no insurance, I had to avoid the cost of an emergency room visit—*at all costs!*

I wanted to avoid the bill that was sure to come from an emergency room visit. But by the time my fiancée, Katie, talked me into going to the hospital, the stuff coming out was no longer liquid; it was more of a black goopy gunk.

Once doctors saw me, I passed out. Dehydrated, with blood sugar levels well over 600 ("Normal" is 100-120), I was in diabetic ketoacidosis. Basically, my blood sugar levels were so high that I had a life-threatening condition that develops when cells in the body are unable to get the sugar (glucose) they need for energy because there is not enough insulin.

The good news: By hydrating with I.V solutions, my blood glucose levels could be brought back down. It would take a while, but they assured Katie everything would be fine. Since she had to work in the morning, with their reassurance, she went home to get some sleep.

Back to the medical alarms…

Obviously my sugar levels were playing crazy with my head. It didn't take me long to realize what a stupid thing

I'd started to do. The seemingly empty emergency room had suddenly come to life like an episode of Chicago MED, with two of the biggest male nurses showing up, one on each side. Now, I'm a pretty big dude — about six feet three inches, 225 pounds. These guys picked me up as if I was a toddler, slammed me on the bed and strapped me down as another nurse inserted a catheter. Lights out! ... Yes, it happens even in Vegas.

Next thing I know I wake up in a private room, with Katie standing next to the bed holding my hand, crying. Oblivious, I ask, "What's going on?"

"It's Sunday. You're in I.C.U. You've been in a coma for three days. The doctors told me they didn't know if you were going to make it—and to start calling your family.

All I could think... *Oh great, how much is this going to cost?*

With every new I.V., I reminded the nurse we did not have the money to pay any of it. I wanted to bail; on the third day I'd had enough. My blood sugar numbers were good. I was over the flu; vitals were normal, but they wanted to keep me for observation.

I had never personally been in the I.C.U. before, but I knew the price tag that comes along with great health care, so I told the nurse I was leaving. I signed a paper saying I was refusing service. Was I making the right decision? I didn't know. All I could think about was the massive bill.

Before leaving, *of course,* we had to stop at billing. I dreaded stepping up to the window. I thought *that* it was going to kill me, as we watched the lady print page after page of charges. I looked at her and said, "I'm sorry ma'am, but there is absolutely no way I'm able to pay this."

Looking at me, she said, "We know; we can help. Here

is the person you need to see." It turns out this hospital that we had wandered into on that desert night was a Catholic hospital, with the support of a Catholic charity. I wish they could have shared that bit of information with me sooner!

In the end, they were able to help cover more than 85 percent of my total bill. I was able to pay off the rest through their payment plan.

I was only twenty-six years old when I was basically dead to the world for three days. And that voice I recall in my brain that made me rise up out of that hospital bed is a constant and daily reminder "It's time to go…"

We are never guaranteed tomorrow. I learned that at a young age. How did this medical crisis influence how I live my life today?

For one, I know today is all we're guaranteed, and I've had the travel bug my whole life. It's in my DNA, as a third generation homesteader who was born into an adventurous logging family. Growing up in Oregon's lush Willamette Valley, three-month-long summer camping trips at the lake with family and friends were common place.

And long road trips were a big deal in the back of Dad's spray-can painted cherry red 1982 Chevy Luv long-bed pick-up truck, with the higher-in-the-back canopy. Down the windy, infamous California Coastline Highway 1 we would go, full of anticipation, on our seventeen-hour drive to Disneyland.

The Internet didn't exist back then—no Google maps or navigation; no cell phone. For blue collar folks like us, our AAA membership was the key to trip planning success; where to stay, points of interest, free hard copy maps and guide books. *What did I want to be when I grew up?* Maybe a vacation planner for triple A!

Truth is, I love to travel—wherever it is! My first chance to visit the East Coast came in 1995 when I graduated from high school. My best friend came from a split family. His Mom lived in Oregon. His Dad lived on the East Coast. Close friends since first grade, he had decided to go to college at UNC at Chapel Hill, and his dad knew this was going to be a monumental change in both of our lives. To help ease the transition, he suggested I come out with Dave for a visit. He invited me to stay a couple weeks at their house on a golf course in Fayetteville, and join them at their timeshare in Myrtle Beach during the week of 4th of July. Pretty upscale for a country boy, but I managed to pay for my plane ticket to make my first big trip, which was a life changing one.

I was in awe of the many firsts: It was the first time I saw the Atlantic Ocean—dramatically different from Oregon's Pacific—and real dolphins, *live,* in the ocean. I got to cruise the strip in an avocado-green 1968 Camero convertible. So cool! And it was the first time I got to bail my best buddy out of jail. Not so cool! It was also my first vacation stay in a timeshare—with ownership that opens up worldwide travel opportunity that stirred my interest to learn more.

Fast forward to 2016, and I'm all grown up—*I think!* And I am one of the "Timeshare Guys" who could write a book on the amazing stories I hear on a daily basis from the owners that use their timeshare.

"Stuff your eyes with wonder, live as if you'd drop dead in ten seconds. See the world."

—Ray Bradbury

Timeshare travel has been a gift for me and my wife, and our two girls. So far, I've traveled to thirty-eight states, British Columbia—and had to hit Tijuana! My wife grew up traveling with her parent's timeshare and saw the value early on in our relationship.

Someone once said *that travel is the only thing you buy that makes you richer*—in life experience, knowledge of people, places and things!

Is it time to go?

Today, what significance does that statement hold for me? Well... I'm still a Type 1 diabetic. That's not going away any time soon—but I don't plan to either! It's a daily struggle to maintain the discipline to help me live life as a healthy diabetic. Many others have a much heavier cross to bear, which helps me keep my own challenges in perspective.

Like buying timeshare, the key with diabetes is to make educated, informed decisions—the payoff is literally life-changing. Being present in life today, living in the only time I can—right now, helps me pay attention, listen to my body, and have a mindset that knows the importance of exercise, diet and healthy liquids—understanding "the bad" of sugar in all forms, and the value of reading labels, to *choose* right. Those are things I can control.

So far, the coma of 2003 was a one-time thing. My last visit to I.C.U. was in 2010. Six years and counting—knowing what signs to look for, I intend to do my best to keep adding time to the clock.

I feel blessed to have had a wake-up call to life at just twenty-six, before I even put a ring on Katie's finger, and before we had two beautiful girls. Now, I do my best to not take a minute of my time here for granted. The coma is a constant reminder for me. "It's time to go... live life and travel!"

We are all here on borrowed time. We never know when our number will be pulled. *Life is God's timeshare.* When my time is up, I want my family and friends to have great memories of our wild adventures and fun times. Those can never be taken away—special moments together, watching colorful fireworks explode over the crashing waves on the sands of Myrtle Beach—a privileged view from the balcony of that penthouse timeshare that took up half of the top of the resort on 4th of July, 1995; flying on Disneyland's Dumbo for the first time, and laughing with arms raised high; a birds-eye view of the New York Skyline from the top of the Empire State building, on a crystal clear night in Manhattan. Seeing the show *Chicago*, live, on Broadway three times. And yes, I confess to some partying on the Las Vegas Strip until the sun comes up.

My wish for you?

Make an investment in living life and creating memories with those you care about and love. When your time comes, and your life flashes before your eyes, rest assured, the time you invested in making memories will live on and last forever.

If you're still here reading this book, you might be missing the point. I'm not sure what you're waiting for… get up!

It's time to go…

Nate Roberts

Nate Roberts is a principal real estate broker licensed in the state of Oregon, who has specialized in timeshare vacation ownership for the past sixteen years. He is one of a very limited number of legitimate brokers who specialize in the resale of timeshare. Vast experience and knowledge in the industry enables him to help owners get the most out of their timeshares. He serves prospective buyers by providing *all* relevant information before buying—a decision he knows will impact the rest of their lives. His passion is to enjoy travel as he builds memories with family and friends, and helping others experience timeshare travel that best fits their goals and lifestyle. Nate is also the owner of Nocturnal Energy, a company that specializes in digital advertising strategies. His expertise is helping business owners "Plug In and Power Up" for massive online exposure for their products and services. Nate invites others to contact him, saying, "I am always looking for the right connections, relationships, business opportunities and partnership prospects—let's connect!"

nocturnalenergy@gmail.com

www.NocturnalEnergy.com

"UNTIL YOU CROSS THE BRIDGE OF YOUR INSECURI-
TIES, YOU CAN'T BEGIN TO EXPLORE THE POSSIBILI-
TIES."

—TIM FARGO

Crossing Bridges

SUSAN GREIF

The fairy tale, "Three Billy Goats Gruff," tells the story of three billy goats trying to cross a bridge to get to the other side—where the meadow is green and plush. However, there is a fierce and cruel troll underneath the bridge who threatens to "gobble them up" as they cross.

So it goes… the first and smallest goat persuades the troll to wait for the next goat who is bigger—and he safely crosses the bridge. Then, the medium-sized goat persuades the troll to wait, once again, because the next goat is even bigger! The troll also allows him to cross. At last, the largest goat comes to the bridge and the ravenous troll jumps on the bridge to devour him. Unfortunately for the troll, the largest goat was huge, and attacks the troll, tossing him over the bridge. As the troll plunges downstream, the largest goat confidently crosses the bridge.

We all have bridges to cross, what we do with the challenges faced in the crossings are our choice. I've had my share of bridges, with plenty of trolls underneath. My hope, in sharing my story is that I can encourage an easier bridge crossing for you.

I remember it well... I began dental school, but quit the day after orientation. My dream of becoming an accomplished doctor came to a quick end in just a matter of hours. Why?

I was raised by traditional parents who survived the horrors of the Holocaust. My parents questioned my choice. "Why do you want to put your hands in someone else's mouth?"

In the meantime, I had also become engaged. Not feeling I could do both, I struggled to make a choice: either focus on my career choice and studies, or focus on marriage and family.

I contemplated my choices for weeks before dental school began. I cried each night with anxiety. On the one hand, I wanted to be an independent, modern woman, yet having been raised by traditional parents, I agonized over the pressure of their strong convictions. They felt, and wanted me to feel, that a woman's place was in the home, to cook, clean and raise children. I silently questioned myself: Was I choosing the male-dominated field of dentistry to quietly rebel against the traditional roles my parents wanted me to pursue?

I weighed my excuses to get out of dental school: Would I have to delay having kids so I could work with formaldehyde infused cadavers? And if I chose to have kids after dental school, would I ever want to return to dentistry? I concluded, dental school wouldn't work, not then anyway.

Instead, over the next seven years, I got married, birthed four children and lost both of my parents. I believe there is a reason for everything in life, and I had no regrets staying home and raising my family, until…

One day I turned to my oldest child, then eight-years-old, and asked her what she wanted to do when she grew up. She responded, "I want to be a mommy and do nothing like you." That not only felt like a dagger in my heart, but brought with it the regrets of deep desires left behind—a twisted, stabbing reminder of the part of me that never expressed itself.

Suddenly, I knew I had to do something more, outside the home, that stood out as more important, to be a strong role model for my daughters. The classes I had been taking in dance, drama, art, writing and photography, were no longer enough to satisfy my doing and learning, or how my daughters perceived me and my role as their mother.

As timing would have it, my local temple created a mission to help the Albanian refugees located in Macedonia during the Balkan War. With my husband's support, I joined the group and brought my camera with me. A reporter from the Jewish Standard, who was on the mission with us, told me if I captured any great photos, he would publish them.

Fortunately, I chose to document our entire journey. With camera in hand, I photographed the emotions that exuded from the war-torn older faces and the innocent youthful faces—the faces told more than words. The camp, run by an Israeli group, used art, music, dance, and play to aid expression and healing for the displaced Muslim refugees.

The Universe has a way of guiding us. But if we don't pay attention, we miss out. I came home, developed my colored, and my black and white photos, which were published in local and foreign newspapers, and in *Lifestyle Magazine*. I was thrilled!

In addition, my photos were displayed at a few art shows, including a museum and a New York City Gallery, with proceeds going to an Albanian group who helped the refugees. The accolades my photos received helped me feel happy and alive—and accomplished.

My real life photographic art was not my husband, not my children; it was authentic expressions of me and my heart. Thinking I had found my calling, I turned to my husband and told him, "I want to be a photo-journalist and travel the world."

My husband, the realist, asked me, "How can you do this with four children, under eight, at home?" He was right. I felt another dream squelched. I resumed my mother-at-home position, following my mother's traditional role. It wasn't a question of my immense love for my husband and children, but there was a creative need within me that they couldn't fill.

When my kids began full school days, I missed time with them. And I felt another void that led to depression. My days seemed empty, so I pursued creative self-healing activities that challenged my mind and body—yoga, meditation, and energy healing. This began an introspective journey that drew me closer to discovering a new creative calling and life purpose. I knew somewhere there was work that would bring joy, and make me feel more complete and accomplished. I soon had an epiphany that came from my love of photography, as well as the healing arts I had learned!

Standing in the darkroom at the International Center of Photography, I watched my black and white images slowly emerge on the paper, as they floated in the developing solution. In no time, the majestic George Washington Bridge became prominent.

This image was part of a series of photos I had taken: images of bridges, windows, doorways, archways—and other images seen through open spaces. My professor walked over to peek at my photo. She examined it, and asked, "What are you waiting for? What do you need to do to get to the other side?"

It made me wonder: How does she know I am trying to figure that out? Because in reality, I was trying... *yearning*... to cross the bridge where I could discover my life's creative purpose on the other side.

Talking this over with a friend, she suggested I apply to the New School in New York City. They offered a certification in Creative Arts Therapies. I considered it. And I also considered going to graduate school to get my masters in Art Therapy, so I contacted some of the New York graduate schools and inquired about the pre-requisites. I was disappointed to learn that all of the undergraduate psychology classes I took in college were obsolete—all would have to be retaken, as well as many of my art classes taken earlier.

Still raising my children, I knew I would have to take my undergraduate class work part time. It would take years! I questioned myself: What if I didn't like art therapy after all? I gave up on the notion of returning to grad school—or pursuing the certification in art therapies.

A few years later, while crying through one of my depressive periods, my husband turned to me and said, "I know what will make you happy... if you worked with children at Bet Elazraki (a children's home in Israel). You could do art work with them."

A light bulb clicked. My heart shot up in response...

it felt exactly right. Finally, I decided to apply to the New School's Creative Arts Therapies (CAT) Program, two years after my friend had first suggested it.

I sat in class knowing that I belonged there. Surrounded by other right-brained people, I was able to create and make neural connections to everything taught. I felt like that annoying kid in the back of the room waving her arm up in the air, gesturing "Ooh, ooh, pick me" or "I know the answer, hello-oh, can't you see my arm?"

During the CAT program at the New School, I interned at the Hudson Guild in Manhattan. I worked with three- to four-year-old children. There was a cute little blond girl who didn't speak, she only grunted and used her body to deflect those classmates who bothered her. Being the mother that I was, I used the skills I was taught from the speech therapist who worked with my children, to see if the little girl could hear, process the information and speak. She was able to.

Eventually, I had her repeat the word and create its action. In time, the little girl finally spontaneously asked me, "Can you wash my hands?" That was the gift we gave each other.

I was so excited for her, and happy to know I was able to make a change in this little girl's life. Her teacher asked me to work one-on-one with her, even though certification interns are prohibited from doing so. After I began, I learned that she had immense fears.

Upon reviewing her records, I read that she was diagnosed with selective mutism; there was an order of protection against her father. We acted out her fears. Teaching her empowering tools, she began to say "no" to those classmates who bothered her, and asked for help from the teachers.

It felt fabulous to have a gift to help her and others.

I became so passionate about what I did that when I approached my bridge, the one I knew I had to cross, I no longer felt threatened by the troll, or the negative self-talk, that seemed to sabotage me and keep me from crossing before.

Amazed—I finally concluded that all my knowledge and experiences had finally integrated into my purpose in this life: being a wife and a mother of four; and with my studies and learning in science, psychology, art, dance, drama, writing—I was integrating a multi-sensory approach to learning. Those, along with the wellness therapies, yoga and energy healing that I practiced were finally being put to good use.

I had become the largest billy goat! I had finally crossed the bridge, leaving the bothersome troll behind! I became a published photographer, illustrator, and now, an author. I learned to take control of the inner critic by confronting it. The result is inner strength and wisdom—and new found self-love and self-respect that keep me walking confidently forward.

It took many years, but I am living a purposeful life. My business, Art Mends Hearts, LLC, is a unique multidisciplinary approach to help and healing that empowers women and children to cross over their bridges, and overcome self-imposed hurdles.

There will always be bridges, with threatening trolls underneath them—your negative self-talk, or inconvenient circumstances, or one excuse or another; those things that try to prevent you from taking that first step, and each step thereafter. Are you ready to cross your bridge? What's holding you back?

Susan Greif

Susan Greif is a "Creative Transformational Expert and Healing Arts Professional," who uses her unique multidisciplinary approach to help women and children find emotional freedom from the ravages of anxiety, depression, trauma, abuse, grief, loss, illness, pain, eating disorders, social behavior and learning disabilities. Her ongoing goal is to see her clients let go of anxieties that keep them feeling paralyzed, powerless, panicked, and in emotional pain. Susan believes that in order to make a change in physical, emotional, and spiritual well-being, clients need to create greater awareness, be willing to see and accept the truth, and bring thoughts to the conscious level—creating clarity. She feels her approach with the expressive arts activates 'subconscious to conscious' quicker than talk therapy, making thoughts and emotions more perceptible. Her purpose is clear—the joy and fulfillment that comes from seeing her clients learn new skills, so they can heal from whatever has them stuck and stopped from crossing their bridge(s). Seeing them learn to make decisions that enable moving forward to living a happier, healthier, and more balanced lifestyle, with a mended heart, is Susan's passion.

artmendshearts@gmail.com

www.artmendshearts.com

"FAITH IS THE BIRD THAT FEELS THE LIGHT WHEN THE DAWN IS STILL DARK."

—RABINDRANATH TAGORE

Who Knew?

SELINA MAITREYA

awoke to a brilliant sunny morning—ready to step forward into my new life. I felt peaceful and excited, and I had absolutely no way of knowing how "new" my life was about to become.

I was happy, and looking forward to a different pace of life. For the past fifteen years, I had been a single mom to my two boys. And to say I worked hard, was a gross understatement.

I believed in doing it all: I was a business consultant to photographers worldwide; I'd written two best-selling books, and had given over one hundred lectures. At home, I cooked dinner nightly, exercised at the gym, and maintained my ten gardens. I went to parent teacher conferences, saved community land with my neighbors, and attended the many important events in my boys' life.

My world was full of love and service to others. I felt supremely grateful for the life *I had created*, and felt blessed as I had always experienced a deep spiritual connection.

My whole-hearted commitment to my spiritual path

had been nourished by my long-term relationship with my spiritual teacher and actualized through my daily life. It has always been important for me to live my spiritual values, using my world as my practice pad. That was my oxygen. That was my fuel.

My spiritual life became my companion. I chose not to have romantic relationships in order to have the time and focus for the development of my spiritual consciousness.

Over time, as my life became an expression of grace and gratitude, I began to hear the call to teach others, which quickly became a deep-seated need. I felt compelled to be a spiritual teacher, and I strived over and over to try to find a way to include this extra commitment into my world.

My life was too full of responsibilities. My brain was so jammed with "to do" lists, I had no *space* to even consider what I was to teach.

Each time I turned to Spirit and asked for help I heard, "Wait." As I listened, I knew I needed to be patient and wait until my boys had grown into lives of their own. As much as I loved my life, that was not what I wanted to hear. Waiting became painful, and endurance, once again became my lesson.

The years passed, and one day standing in my kitchen in the house that I loved so very much, I heard the words: "It's time to sell your house, it's time to move."

With my boys now in college and graduate school, I replayed Spirit's words, and I realized how perfect the timing was.

I chose New York City as the place to start my new life. I was born in New York, but had lived in Massachusetts for the last forty years.

Now I was going to return and begin life anew.

A few months after making the decision to sell my house, I gave a lecture in Bogota, Columbia. There, I met a photographer who owned an apartment in New York that he offered to rent to me. With a place to live, I felt my decision was confirmed when my house went on the market and sold in one day. Everything was falling into place!

I had two weeks between my house closing and moving to New York City, and I decided to visit friends I had not seen in years. This was to be my first opportunity to relax. Finally, I could take a breath after years of hard work.

Now here I was, waking at a local hotel, two days before my house closing.

My belongings were on their way to New York, my house was empty and I looked forward to cleaning it for the very last time.

Getting into my convertible, I put the top-down and looked up into the sky, took a deep breath and thanked the universe for this new day.

This was it; I was beginning my new life.

I arrived at a traffic light I had driven through a thousand times. As I sat at the light, the sky was getting gray, so I reached down, hit the button and put the top up on my car.

With the green light, I drove into the intersection—and suddenly I heard a thunderous noise over my left shoulder. I turned to look in the direction of the sound. I saw the horrified look on a woman's face, and then in a flash, my car filled with the most brilliant light.

Immediately, all there was—and all I was—was light. I knew I was dying.

I thanked the universe for my magnificent life and said that if this was my time, I was ready. Then, I ceased to exist. I had no thoughts. I had no feelings. I was nothing.

There are no words to describe the experience of non-existence. To call it peaceful is a crass understatement. To say it is the place of calm is thoroughly inadequate.

I'm not sure how long I was in this non-existent state before I returned to physical awareness. I heard a voice, quietly and clearly say, "Turn to the right." I saw a pole in front of me and turned the wheel of my car.

Eventually my car stopped and it was clear I had experienced a car accident.

After the Jaws of Life extricated me from my damaged convertible, I realized I had no scratches, bruises or broken bones. I was released from the hospital in a few hours. I was shaken, sore and very confused, but felt totally blessed as I had been spared.

I learned from a state trooper that the car that hit me was dragging me directly into a pole that would have killed me—except—according to witnesses, I had turned away and in the last few seconds and landed three inches from the pole.

Clearly, beginning my new life would need to wait. I couldn't drive. I had no car. My house was sold, so I had no home.

As the days continued on, I became foggier and less able to function. It quickly became clear that something was very wrong. Walking was a major effort. I was unable to do the simplest of tasks. My dear friends cared for me; I couldn't cook or write an email. Fatigue was overwhelming me and I was unable to tolerate any light or noise

The diagnosis from my neurologist was a major brain injury. How long would the healing of my brain take? Who knew? It could be weeks, months, or years—or perhaps, I would never be the same again. I had no idea when I would be able to work, write, or teach again.

While the news was bleak, I was experiencing a miracle. I had access to a place of exquisite quiet. My heart was wide open. I continually felt the sense of true Oneness. I had no fear. I saw no judgment. Though my thoughts were muffled and hard to access, when I closed my eyes, I felt directly connected to the peace, light and quiet that had filled my car throughout the accident.

During this time, the Masters of the Oneness came to me and told me not to worry—explaining that this experience was the answer to my prayers. This was to be my path to being a spiritual teacher. My life had been so full that I had to be taken completely out of my life in order to experience it as intended. *New* required—"rewiring my frequencies" and "downloading" the information I was to teach. I discerned from Spirit that the days ahead would be different from what I had planned. Surrender and trust would be my tools—and I was to know that all I needed would be provided.

I showed up each day. I continued to keep my awareness in my front pocket, and remained receptive to allowing my "new" life to unfold. I continuously and willingly surrendered. Regardless of how difficult my circumstances became, I never had a moment of fear, doubt or uncertainty.

The Masters asked that l refer to my experience, not as an "accident," but as an event experienced to receive the greatest teaching of my life.

It's been three years. As I write this story, I'm living in my apartment in New York City. My new life hasn't come without challenges, but the miracles exist beside them.

The significance of my experience is that I continue to surrender and co-create with the Masters. I stopped directing my life, and am completely open to their guidance. This one shift has dramatically changed my world—genuinely creating a *new life*, a new me.

On the physical and neurological end, my brain is almost healed—I'm able to create, write, and teach. I am amazed at my recovery process.

Although, I no longer drive, I can do many of the ordinary daily activities that were so difficult after the *event*. I ride on trains, sit in crowded restaurants, go to museums, and walk in parks. I continue to rest and meditate every day, and have worked myself up to a six hour work day.

On the spiritual front, my tears flow thinking about the Holy experiences I have witnessed—miracle after miracle, parallel difficulty and hardship. Challenging situations in my life are now opportunities to surrender more deeply to Spirit's direction.

I live in gratefulness for the financial pathways, and supportive people, that continuously appear. I can't express enough gratitude for the information that Spirit has provided me that I now share as a spiritual teacher.

Most importantly, what has become clear to me is that I am a very different person. *Who knew that the woman that entered her car in 2013, expecting to have a new life, would become an entirely new being!* After years and years of directing and orchestrating everybody else's world, I am now the co-creator of my own, leaving *striving* and *wanting* behind. Settled deep within me, is peace, calm, and connection to the source that showed up in my car as all encompassing light, which has never left my side.

Selina Maitreya

For over thirty years Selina Maitreya has been a spiritual student, studying many philosophies and spiritual practices. Drawn to the simple yet powerful idea that *we are all ONE*—that our natural inheritance is LOVE, and that our actions affect every single energy entity, Selina began to make her daily life her practice, committing to responding to all events and beings from love. After a successful 30 plus year career as a guide to visual professionals, lecturing over 100 times and authoring two books, Selina answered the call to serve as a teacher. Selina is committed to reacquainting others with their true authenticity. Her work, "Practical Spirituality" refers to living our spiritual values, not simply studying or talking about them. Selina works one-on-one with individuals, and with groups, empowering them to awaken and re-connect to their higher wisdom through their daily actions and choices.

Selina has been interviewed on numerous radio programs and blogs, and her inspirational teachings have been received globally.

For more information on Selina and "Practical Spirituality" go to:

www.selinamaitreya.com

www.facebook.com/PracticalSpiritualityWithSelina/

"Darkness and fear are the Great Awakeners. In facing my fears, I find my freedom." "Ask yourself, 'Did I overcome fear and learn how to love?'"

—Class 28 Meditation, Shifting From Fear to Love

From Silence To Soul Song

ANGELA ALCANTAR

Everything feels like it is falling apart. Most of what I have known myself to be no longer seems relevant—meaning and vibrancy have slipped away. I am turning into a liquefied mess, living a life without consistency or borders; a personal metamorphosis is taking place.

What is happening? *I want to know who I am.* Life feels thorny—and confused. And then one day, after a lengthy stretch of feeling restless and uncomfortable, I notice something has changed within me. I begin to feel more solid. Not only am I more sturdy and strong, an inner lightness I hadn't known before, prevails. With this lightness comes a deeper sense of joy—a profound sense of self. My soul has a song to sing and it can no longer be repressed.

But prior to this, when and why did I start feeling confused and restless? It began when my thoughts and feelings of depression wouldn't leave me alone—January 2008. Despondency had me asking: *Why is this happening again? Why do I feel so awful? I can't do this! I don't want to get out of bed. I don't want to go to work. Sleep is my only friend, especially during the dark winter months. My pattern of depression starts with the autumn clouds, and begins to turn around in March, when the light from the sun returns, and its healing warmth is felt.*

A continuous flow of unresolved thoughts interrupted my sound thinking: *Do I have seasonal affective disorder? Am I really depressed? I can't be. I'm too successful to be depressed. I know better. I have a degree in psychology. I should be able to reason my way out of this: But... I'm not really tired, I just don't want to interact with my husband. Is that it? I wasn't sure. Was I subconsciously using sleep and work to avoid interacting with him?*

My thoughts kept me out of balance: *I need to see someone... I am going to have to start taking medication. I have to do something!* One thing I knew for sure, I needed to stop this unhealthy pattern; it was taking a toll on me. I wanted to feel good. I wanted to feel happy. But, how?

My body began to confirm what my subconscious already knew. Digestive problems were frequent—bloating and discomfort—and out of the blue, I would wake up vomiting, with no obvious cause. Tests were done, but to no avail. I kept telling myself, *I have to do something!* I started acupuncture treatments, twice a month, and it was then that I began to heal. An inner strength that I had buried somewhere deep in the caverns of my soul began to emerge.

The unfolding of *truth*—suddenly in November, 2010, I blurted out to my acupuncturist, "I know what my problem is. I don't want to be married anymore." This was a surprise to me and a major relief. . .

So began mirror work, affirmations, and a daily gratitude journal—my first baby steps on the journey of transformation. To be honest, at first, I couldn't even look at myself in the mirror, but stayed committed. The affirmations were surprisingly powerful: "I love and approve of myself. I am safe." I would also tell myself, "I love you," twenty times a day, while looking at myself in the mirror.

I want you to know, the first couple of days I could barely whisper "I love you." And I merely imagined myself standing in front of a mirror. The next couple of days I pushed myself to stand in front of the mirror, even if I couldn't look myself in the eyes.

Why is it so hard for some of us to love ourselves? To be honest with you, when asked, "Do you love yourself?" I couldn't respond with, "Yes, I love myself." … yet I didn't know why I felt that way. I now know, I had been denying my soul's song because I wasn't able to love and accept my *true self.*

> *"Instead of avoiding those things we fear, we start pro-actively selecting those ways of being, thinking and acting that most efficiently take us toward what we consciously want."*
> —Marsha Sinetar, *Elegant Choices, Healing Choices*

My soul began to compose a song as I gained freedom and reestablished my voice and self-worth. Though it was difficult, choosing to divorce enabled me to flourish—slowly unfolding like the petals of a rose, as healthy self-love and self-acceptance restored and nourished my very being. I discovered my inner voice; I could breathe and I learned how to trust it. My previous unrest had propelled me on a journey of self-discovery and soul transformation. My soul could now sing a song of authenticity.

My journey to feeling better, to finding joy, to loving myself consisted of four lessons. The time had come for me to courageously take the necessary steps to make my soul's desires a reality.

Growing Pains of Transformation

> *"Moving beyond fear only happens if and as we give ourselves permission to feel our fears and anxieties. The absolute first-step in resolving these uncomfortable feelings is to admit we have them..."*

—Marsha Sinetar, *Elegant Chices, Healing Choices*

How *does* a person work through the unpleasant parts of personal transformation? Transformation is uncomfortable—it causes growing pains, uneasiness, doubt and fear—especially the fear of the unknown.

A fundamental aspect of transformation is recognizing that these seemingly negative feelings, interwoven in our life circumstances that demand changes within us, are on our side. *We can learn how to find comfort in the discomfort.*

By leveraging the power of these feelings, we are propelled into the greatest version of ourselves—the version we are meant to be. Moving through our fear, rather than avoiding it, helps us to embrace it, and we experience new learning and growth. *Our souls are allowed to sing their songs!*

We may feel discomfort or constriction in our body—often around our heart center. Some of us become physically ill, experiencing a variety of other health issues. For me, my stomach pains were a sign that I needed a change. I realized these pains were serving me, once I knew how to recognize them—and when I learned how to breathe through them, slow and steady like an expanding balloon, my life began to change for the better.

The process of transformation, making changes we might rather avoid, and trying things we are unfamiliar with—stretch us like the rubber on an expanding balloon: *I will try a new way of behaving. I will try a new way of interacting. I will try a new way of problem solving.* When I do, I am pleasantly surprised by the results—my soul sings with joy and satisfaction!

Becoming Okay with the Unknown

One day, I was sharing my journey of transformation with a friend, over a glass of wine. We were discussing how in the past, I would plan, control and force things to happen, but would always end up dissatisfied with the end result.

There is comfort in knowing what is going to happen. However, my need to know limited my ability to see the possibility of *what could be.* As we were discussing how we avoid fear by demanding clarity and certainty, I spoke these words, "I would rather see spiders than *not* know what is going to happen."

Now you must understand, even the thought of spiders makes me ill, there is little else in this world that I dislike more; however, my fear of the unknown was even greater!

You know that expression, "Be careful what you ask for"? Well, over the next three days, I saw the biggest spiders I have ever seen in my house. Spotted crawling in the bathroom sink, on my bedroom wall, and in my tortilla warmer—they were everywhere! My distaste for spiders helped me realize I would rather learn how to become comfortable with the unknown—*rather* than to see spiders. I kid not! Thank you, Universe! Thank you, spiders!

"Life begins at the end of your comfort zone."

—Neale Donald Walsch

If I stay in the place of the known, where it is comfortable because I know what to do and I know what to expect, I will keep getting the same results. When I move beyond my comfort zone, oh yes, it feels uncomfortable *because* I am growing—refusing to live my life in fear.

"You have to take risks. We will only understand the miracle of life fully when we allow the unexpected to happen."

—Paulo Coelho

Learning How to Allow

Part of becoming okay with the unknown is learning the power of *allowing* life to unfold rather than "making" things happen. The Taoist concept of allowing is known as Wu-Wei. Ted Kardash, Ph.D., explains Wu-Wei as natural order; the whole; life interconnected. In its natural order, life is spontaneous and effortless; life simply flows through us because it is the right action, appropriate to its time and place, and serves a purpose of greater harmony and balance. This includes trusting our own bodies, our own thoughts and our own emotions. We learn to trust, and we believe that the environment will provide all of the support and guidance necessary. This trust is developed through watchfulness and quietness of mind.

By observing, by quieting my mind, I have learned that when I feel myself being stretched outside my comfort zone, my first response is to take control and figure it out—to solve the problem so I can alleviate the discomfort. What I have learned is that in order to transform I have to do things differently.

Instead of seeking to control, I simply notice the discomfort and I allow it to be. I wait to respond, trying my best NOT to figure IT out. I ALLOW myself to be present for whatever is in front of me. I have faith that the answer will reveal itself because I believe I am fully supported and guided by the Universe. *I do not have to figure it out. I do not have to solve it. I do not need to force a resolution.*

> *"When I run after what I think I want, my days are a furnace of stress and anxiety; if I sit in my own place of patience, what I need flows to me, and without pain. From this I understand that what I want also wants me, is* looking for me and attracting me. There is a great secret here *for anyone who can grasp it."*
>
> —Rumi

Self-Care is Self-Love

Perhaps most importantly, through learning to love myself, I have come to understand the absolute necessity of self-care. I intentionally do things that bring me freedom and wellness—and ultimately satisfaction and joy. Dance, acupuncture, hiking, and soaking in hot springs—all nourish my soul song!

Today, I encourage you—to make time to do those special things that bring *you* health and wellness—nurture *your* soul song. Blessings!

Angela Alcantar

Angela Alcantar, founder of The True You 2day, LLC, is dedicated to lifelong learning. As a teacher, coach and encourager, her clear purpose is to empower others to live an authentic life from their soul's center. "Let your soul's song, sing!" Angela passionately seeks *truth*, not only for herself, but she looks for ways in which to help others do the same for themselves. She does not use *one* method, but is always creative as she adapts her work to each individual situation. She believes there is a power and a presence in the Universe that is for good—and that each person can use this energy to create more good, love and satisfaction in their own lives. Angela welcomes you to contact her at:

thetrueyou2day@gmail.com

thetrueyou2day.com

"The moments that hold mystery, whether dressed in pain or wonder, wait to be treated with respect and sincerity; as if a message was carved in stone for you before you were born, and a storm has washed it ashore just in time, and you need all the help you can get to decipher its meaning. And we will be found by our teachers repeatedly—be they the moon, the thief, or the tiger—until we can uncover their meaning."

—Mark Nepo, "Opening The Gift"

Spider Is Your Grandmother

BOBBY LEE

I was blessed to have two parents that I loved very much and that I know loved me. This does not mean that they always treated me with loving kindness, or that I never questioned that they loved me, or that they always acted in kind loving ways. On the contrary, they sometimes were thoughtless, not considerate, and even at times abusive. They were treating me in the only way they knew, and in the same way that they had been raised.

My father was an army officer, much affected by the horror he had witnessed, and the deaths of the men he had led in fighting against the Nazi's in World War II. As an officer, he taught that ladies were always to be treated with respect and kindness. This was contradicted by his actions of anger and disrespect leading to physical abuse of my mother, me and my four brothers, when he was drinking alcohol.

Until I was fifteen years old, I was very afraid of my father, and it would be fair to say I tried to avoid him when he was drinking. Somehow the lessons taught of how to behave, were every so often contradicted by the actions of my parents. So I grew up feeling it was my job to defend my mother, and all women I knew from physical abuse—and felt it was my place to treat women with gentle, thoughtful kindness in my relationships with them.

I felt very close to my mother, even though when drinking, she made poor decisions that put me in a position of needing to act like an adult—among adults who were acting like inconsiderate out of control children. Growing up, I did not even think about the fact that it was a complete reversal of roles, or did I doubt that I had the ability to take charge and have some control in situations that were spiraling out of control. I had no idea where this confident thinking originated. I felt some sort of reliable power and wisdom to draw upon, during the destructive outbursts and behaviors within our house.

After passing through some turbulent years as a teenager, I began to search for the meaning of my life. *Why was I born? What had I come to this earth to do?* And *why,* when I was searching for my spiritual home, in each new church, did I run into the "Except For's?"

Everyone is welcome here *except for* those who are_____; *except for* those who have_____; *except for* those who have not _____; *except for* those who believe_____). You can fill in the blanks.

I found "The Precious Beloved" in beauty, in nature, in the flowers, the sunsets, and in my heart. I could not believe in a God who loved everyone "Except for…"

My heart proved trustworthy when it led me to accept and understand that God and love were synonyms—and if God was omnipresent, then God was also in me, and simultaneously, then love was in me—and the truth then, was that God and love were in everyone!

I did not understand who these "Except For's" could be in God's eyes, but I knew that the Higher Power that resonated with me could only be one that was for everyone, one who had no "Except For's."

Once I had this life-changing revelation at the age of twenty-five, I went to my father and put my arms around him. I gave him a big bear hug. I held on tight as he struggled to get away. I said, "Dad, I love you. I will always love you. Nothing you have done or will ever do can make me not love you."

As he began to cry in my arms I told him that although he and I had some different values, I never meant to make him look or feel bad, or to disrespect him. In 1965, when my oldest brother, Captain James G. Lee, was twenty-nine, he was killed in Vietnam. My father, being a retired army officer himself, felt obligated to support the war effort. I felt obligated to do the exact opposite—oppose the war and speak out against it.

I shared that in order to respect myself, I needed to follow my own heart and my own inner guidance. I appreciated his opinion, but at the same time, I hoped he could appreciate in me that he had raised a strong man who would follow his own convictions. I then said, " Would you like to go to the local bar and have a beer?" We did, and from then on my dad and I were very close.

As I pursued my spiritual searching for an understanding of life, and my roles in it, I came upon a small church called the Alaska Church of Religious Science.

The first Sunday service I attended, the minister, Rev. Nancee Sweeney Padzieski, said that if something or someone in your life was bothering you, it would not go away out of anger, by frustration or by hate. If you wanted to be free of something you would need to *love it*. I completely agreed, and for the next several years Rev. Nancee became my teacher.

She taught me to meditate. During a silent meditation in her center, I had a personal experience of recognizing the deep love that had always surrounded me—and the strong influence of the female teachers I had encountered in my life. Several of the ladies in that congregation told me that they admired the way I balanced my feminine and masculine sides. I had not given much thought to masculine/feminine traits, but it was true that I had many strong teachers of both sexes.

One of the Hermetic Principles (based upon the writings attributed to Hermes Trismegistus), is that everything is both masculine/feminine. Feminine does not require weak and masculine does not require strong. Life is a balance of all things; not the middle of a scale of a particular trait, but the harmony of all the traits.

Everything is perfect. My belief that God is perfect and that God is omnipresent (everywhere all the time), leads me to conclude that if God is present all the time *in everything* then those things must be perfect.

I often look at things as they appear and say, "Wow! I did not know perfection looked like this." You see, Spirit sees things from the *whole perspective* while my view is limited by what my eyes see right in front of me, right now. Knowledge and understanding of God's love and unlimited perspective helps us in all things.

When my mother died, it left a large void in my life. Since we lived in Alaska, it was months after my mother died before she could be buried. Four months later, the ground was finally thawed enough for a burial. Afterwards, Edna, a good friend who is profoundly conscious, offered to help with my grieving process. One of the many healing modalities she shares is her ability to drum and chant. Edna is a First Nation person from Yukon Territory, Canada, and assists people in finding their path in life.

Edna knew how the loss of my mother affected me, and she guided me in how to deepen my grieving process, and focus on *being* in the present. She led me into her sacred space, where I sat on a deer skin she had prepared. The scent of sage and sweet grass was prevalent, and the air itself somehow felt elevated.

As she began to drum and chant, Edna told me to relax, close my eyes, and allow whatever came into my mind to pass on through, but to be aware and look for the presence of three animals. She said the presence of "three of the same" would indicate that they were to be my spirit guides, and when they appeared I should follow them.

I closed my eyes and began to relax into the thoughts passing behind my closed eyes. Edna's rhythmic chant and the resonance of the drum created the sensation of vibrations penetrating deeply into my body, and I grew very relaxed. Then, I felt a sensation on my leg—and looking down, I saw one of the largest spiders I had ever seen as it crawled up my leg.

Not wanting to lose the moment, I tried to ignore the spider and kept looking for the three spirit guides. The spider continued on, and once it reached my folded arms, it climbed from my leg to my arm and continued upwards. It was not a heavy sensation, but it was difficult to keep a focus within my mind for my three animals, while feeling this spider climbing up my arm. Once it reached my shoulder, it walked up my neck, and onto my chin, and then across my face.

I thought, 'How can I find my spirit guides while my attention is on this spider?'

All at once, I saw my mother's eyes. Looking deeply into her eyes, I forgot the spider though I could still feel it. After moments of deeply looking into my mother's eyes, I felt this intense love, knowledge and strength reflected there.

Next, I saw my grandmother's eyes, my mother's mother. She was looking back into my eyes as if she could see everything in my life. Somehow, this stern and loving set of eyes was *seeing everything about me.* I suddenly felt this intense connection to wisdom and understanding that was beyond anything I had ever known.

Edna continued to drum and chant—all the while this spider was walking down my neck on the other side—and even so, I was supposed to be seeking three animal spirit guides. During this, all I saw were my grandmother's eyes.

Once again, I unexpectedly saw a different set of female eyes, which I realized were my great-grandmothers. Again, the intensity of her gaze seemed to see into my very soul—it was mesmerizing. I could sense deep communication, as if it was taking place on a cellular level, innate, without words being spoken.

I lost track of time, and lost track of trying to find the three animal spirit guides I sought on this journey. And again the eyes changed into yet another set of eyes, and then again another, and layer after layer of female eyes appeared, all with a sense of deep connection. Some I knew, some I didn't.

Significant awareness of being influenced and taught by these powerful women became very clear to me—each one had been part of the very creation of my being.

As this epiphany was going on, the spider continued on down my leg, and finally crawled off. All the time I was thinking that the spider had caused me to miss my opportunity to find the spirit guides. Simultaneously, Edna concluded her chanting, and silence filled the space. After a few minutes Edna softly asked "Do you want to share about your spirit guides?"

I said, "To tell the truth, I never found the three animal spirits that were to be my guides. As you began chanting a single spider climbed up and across my body and I was distracted."

"Oh…" Edna said, "Spiders are your grandmothers. In my culture we never harm spiders because they bring the wisdom of the grandmothers."

My spirit guide had come to me, but in a way I had not expected. Goosebumps covered my body as the awareness of what had just transpired began to set in. From that day until now, I have never harmed a spider.

Bobby Lee

Bobby Lee is a Religious Science minister with a deep appreciation of life. Bobby was raised in Alaska, raced the Iditarod Sled Dog Race, bred championship dogs, and lived on a homestead in the backwoods. He worked in many Alaska villages and has in depth knowledge of life and construction north of the Arctic Circle. He helped design and build sewer and water systems, landfills, septic lagoons and roads in many Alaska villages. He has a deep love and respect for Native Alaskans and worked with them primarily on their projects. He is in awe of their skills as subsistence hunters and gatherers. As an adult, Bobby found a deep spiritual calling; through it, he experienced amazing stories of change and second chances for living a loving life. He is the founding minister of the Center for Spiritual Living Cottage Grove, in Oregon, and his personal ministry is known as SpreadLove.

Contact Bobby at:

loydrlee@msn.com

www.facebook.com/BobbyLeeSpreadLove/

"Every living being is an engine geared to the wheelwork of the universe. Though seemingly affected only by its immediate surroundings, the sphere of external influence extends to infinite distance."

—Nikola Tesla

Opportunities are Disguised as Problems

COLETTE MARIE STEFAN

A lot of shifts, personal and universal, have sailed under the bridge since I chose to follow my heart and embark upon on my journey into shifting energy and remote (long distance) healing through what I refer to as H.S. N. (Higher Self Network). Over the last decade, I have been blessed to connect with the finest mentors, work with amazing colleagues, clients, students—and my radio audience and participants at seminars and live demonstrations in Europe, Egypt and North America. It is my pleasure to share life-transforming information that empowers others to tune into their intuition, find creative solutions to their problems and embrace their authentic desires.

As radio host of "The Truth is Funny… shift happens," and co-founder of "Energetic Upgrade" seminars, the EUp Foundation on-line program, and creator/artist of "Tails from the Vector," an oracle featuring paintings and energy correcting cards—I've seen impressive results. But it wasn't always this way!

Looking back, the choices that I made when major

events, such as birth and death and the trauma of physical pain, divorce—and more—along with seemingly insignificant events—all have put me on the fast track to accessing my potential to make my life and the lives of those around me better.

This is done by identifying underlying weaknesses in our energy field, enabling the central nervous system to remove energetic blocks, which in-turn strengthens their heart connection to their authentic desires.

There are definitive moments in all people's lives that direct them to make soul decisions through what may seem like insignificant everyday choices; yet these very choices will have a profound effect on the direction in which their lives will go.

Over the years, I have had many people say to me, "*I could never be as intuitive as you.*" This is absolutely true, because I am intuitive in my own way, but so are you! Just as athletic ability runs in some families, my family on both sides tend to have a strong intuitive connection. I chose to put mine into practice and hone my perception for strong insight. And as you think about it, there are abilities and tendencies that run within you and your family.

There is no secret to being intuitive. We all are! Many people who are highly intuitive are accused of being overly sensitive; however, if you use your sensitivity wisely, it becomes an effective tool to stay aligned energetically, such as being *spontaneous, insightful, discerning, sensitive.* How does a person know they are intuitive?

Our attitude, as we navigate troubled waters, plays a major factor in the outcome of the ongoing story of our life, and the development of our intuition. Each of us is unique, so as a matter of course, so is our journey. And along the way, each person can choose to begin developing intuition.

My own introduction to it was not a gentle nudge—instead it was done in the style of eagles and dragons, where the fledglings are pushed out of their nest, high up on a cliff, to rise above or fall to their deaths. And it was only fitting that my dad, Maurice Joseph LePage was the catalyst! He was an entrepreneur by nature and somewhat impatient. He used to say, "Shift! Or get off the pot!" (… or something to that effect!)

At the age of sixty-eight, my dad collapsed at home, and became paralyzed from head to toe, unable to breathe on his own. Upon admission to the hospital, he was kept overnight for observation and in the morning fell again. In the afternoon, my uncle found him blue and unresponsive in his room. He was resuscitated and taken to intensive care where the diagnosis eventually came back as Guillain-Barré Syndrome.

He held out for over a year, making decisions about his business by blinking his right eye, yes or no. My dad used to joke that the Guillain-Barré diet was the only diet that had ever worked for him, *but he did not recommend it!* He lost over one hundred pounds as he worked to regain his ability to breathe, walk, talk and eat again.

During the time he was in and out of the hospital, he had a tracheostomy that was eventually removed, then replaced when he was still unable to breathe on his own.

Unfortunately, he contracted MRSA infection (Methicillin-resistant Staphylococcus aureus) at the hospital; everyone had to gown, glove and mask themselves every time they entered and left his room. Besides making it hot and itchy for visitors, this awful infection made it inconvenient for hospital staff to look after him, severely impacting the quality of his care.

Over time, I recognized that my dad and I were slowly reversing parenting roles. At that time I was working full time, raising two daughters, often as a single parent because my husband worked away from home for weeks at a time. I did my best to get to the hospital every day, raise awareness with hospital staff about his care, and at the same time, tried to give my daughters some semblance of a happy "normal" life. It was exhausting!

The hospital had given up on my dad, but I refused to! I fought the system to have my dad sent to a rehabilitation center, as he fought to maintain his dignity. Once he received proper care, he made very quick progress. He was soon up using the toilet again and proudly doing laps around the gym. Eventually he was able to be home, off and on.

During the last week of his life, he was back in hospital—and begged me to please "just shoot him." He pointed out that if he were a horse people would have put him out of his misery. Visitors would ask my dad if he had seen the doctor yet, and he would jokingly reply, "Yes, I have seen Dr. Phil on TV," during the times when his actual doctor did not make it in to see him. The no-resuscitation order that was supposed to be in effect *was not signed* and they attempted to resuscitate him against his wishes.

The news came the day before my parent's forty-fourth wedding anniversary; I was jarred from my sleep at 4:00 a.m. by a hysterical call from my mom. The hospital had called; Dad had passed. I threw on my clothes, drove over to pick Mom up and take her to the hospital. She leapt out of the car and ran into the building before I could stop her.

The nurses allowed my mom to see him—her husband, the father of her children, with intubating equipment still forced down his throat—his eyes wide open in a far from peaceful stare. When I witnessed the horror deep within my mother's eyes as she stared down at him, in my heart, I knew that there absolutely had to be a better way to look after people than this.

The system in Canada clearly was not equipped to handle an oversupply of patients and an undersupply of caregivers. There were good people working at the hospital, and there were also people who clearly were not following their purpose as caregivers.

Our family, like most others, has been impacted and influenced by medical care given during illness and catastrophic life events. It was only five weeks later that my niece, returning from the West Edmonton Mall after a last hurrah with three of her friends before starting university, was in a head-on collision with a drunk driver. The girl who was driving was killed, along with the very inebriated driver of the other car. My niece was revived at the scene, stabilized and rushed to the hospital where she underwent several hours of surgery.

If there is such a thing as hell, that night was it. After receiving the phone call from my brother-in-law at midnight, we picked up my sister from work and made the long, arduous journey to Saskatoon from Regina, Saskatchewan. My niece arrived by ambulance shortly later, and so began the vigil during surgery. We watched the mom, who had lost her daughter, go to the morgue to identify her child. The pain etched on her face upon her return, is forever imprinted in my mind.

We rejoiced when the doctors informed us that my niece had survived the surgery. But, she was severely brain damaged, and full recovery was not expected. My sister, her mom, absolutely refused to accept this fate for her, and immediately took steps to change it. She contacted a remote healer who at that time was a teenager living in British Columbia. He energetically tuned in to my niece's energy via her photograph as she lay in Intensive Care in Saskatoon, Saskatchewan, recovering from her injuries. He is now a holistic doctor.

The medical doctors call my niece a "medical miracle." She went on to attend university, continued her modeling career, married, and is the mother of two daughters. Most importantly, her true, beautiful essence still shines from within.

After witnessing her miraculous recovery, I had absolutely no doubt that remote healing is possible—and I wanted to know if I could do it. Since then, I have learned that everyone is capable of remote healing if they apply themselves and follow their inner guidance as to how to develop their intuition.

Life is not fair, but you can benefit from hard circumstances! The people and events you encounter are not random. Every encounter brings opportunity to *shift* your life into a new direction. Challenges are opportunities disguised as problems—when you choose to look for windows of opportunity.

My dad and niece began my journey into the world of energy healing. I have discovered this—not to be limited in my thinking. Information equals energy for positive change! Pay attention to people and events! Ancestral, astrological and planetary influences are all factors that shape our lives.

Most people are unaware of the impact these external forces have on their day-to-day lives and are left wondering, "What the E.F. (External Forces) happened? The "E.Fs"

(External Forces) are subtle and hard to detect because they shake our equilibrium, leaving us to worry about the "what I.Fs" (Internal Forces).

What if this or that happens? The problem is never what people THINK it is! Creative solutions to counteract the problem—and come to us through intuitive insight. Once energetic weaknesses are identified and shifted, people are able to accelerate and expand along with the universe. Unapplied information is just a tool that is not being used. Applying the information I have learned has given my energetic shifts a powerful torque and spin.

I've seen surprising results: children diagnosed with autism and other spectrum disorders living productive lives, people losing weight and shaping their bodies with ease, patients diagnosed with a fatal disease returning to health, infertile mothers giving birth, limbs being repaired that were damaged for years, improvements in business and finances… there are no limitations. It makes my heart sing!

You are a gift! We all are! Follow your heart, put your intuition into practice, take consistent steps of action and the universe will take care of the rest.

Colette Marie Stefan

Colette Marie Stefan is a magical speaker, author and artist, with a great sense of humor, who shares universal, life-transforming information to provide results that will inspire you to soar with her to new heights (in the way of the dragons) at seminars around the globe. She has been the featured guest on many radio shows and tele-summits as well as captivating the airwaves with her hit radio show "The Truth Is Funny... shift happens," as an open invitation for her audience to call in and experience the *joy of shift*. Colette is the author of her long awaited book, *The Truth Is Funny... shift happens...* (stuff you wish your mom had known to tell you). Warning! If you prefer the status quo and you are not interested in improving every aspect of your life... this book may trigger the shift out of you!

Colette co-founded state of the art Energetic Upgrade Seminars and the EUp Foundation program, with her colleague Marc Kettenbach in 2014 and just recently, unleashed her dragons... "Tails From The Vector"... an oracle expressed through her powerful paintings, as well as a beautiful deck of energy correcting cards—a project that has been percolating on the back burner for the last decade. To learn more about Colette, visit:

www.thetruthisfunny.com

colettestefan@gmail.com

"WHAT IS DEFERRED IS NOT AVOIDED."

—SIR. THOMAS MORE

The Unexpected Laminectomy

VERONICA R. LYNCH, PH.D.

It's been said, "Just because the process hurts, it doesn't mean the results won't be beautiful." It was Thanksgiving night, 2014, at our wellness retreat center and vacation home, in the low country of South Carolina. I was standing, washing dishes, and looking out the kitchen window after a wonderful seven course meal, when I began to feel excruciating pain.

This pain was in my lower back, and it radiated below my knees, and down to the calves and ankles of both my legs. This was not only shocking and surprising, but somewhat embarrassing because we had guests for the holiday weekend and I knew I would not be able to fully engage with them.

I finally had to reveal the painful new discovery to my guests, who concluded that it must be sciatica. They readily gave me exercises, similar to yoga postures, to help relieve the pressure. Needless to say, I found little relief. However, I continued with the suggested exercises, in addition to my usual workouts and stretches for months, but to no avail.

I didn't know what I was going to do. With the many months that had passed, I felt impatient, knowing I couldn't spend the rest of my life not being able to walk or stand in comfort.

In June, 2015, I returned home to New York City, my home residence, to see my primary care physician for a referral to a neurologist.

After examination, he suggested I begin physical therapy sessions, in conjunction with acupuncture, massage, and chiropractic sessions.

My calendar was full of professional activities to be accomplished, but I knew correcting this physical condition had to take priority. As a health coach and owner of my own wellness and retreat center in the low country of Beaufort, South Carolina, I'd have to rearrange all dates at the center, and pray that I could find relief and be able to quickly get back to my daily routines of teaching and counseling.

By September, 2015, I had to return to South Carolina. It wasn't long after arriving there, that I was rushed to urgent care due to continued excruciating lower back pain. Again, I was given a different medication for pain, and was referred to see a spine specialist. After x-rays and an MRI, he confirmed that I had spinal stenosis, which he advised could be managed with pain medication.

Showing me a mock-up of a spinal column, he explained that I was born with a small spinal canal, which over time had become compressed and made it difficult for the nerves to flow freely, resulting in lower back pain. Along with the prescribed pain medication, he ordered a back brace and referred me to physical therapy.

After six months of different specialists in South Carolina and New York City and ongoing chiropractic and physical therapy sessions, I felt no real relief. Again, I was referred to another specialist for an electromyography, which confirmed that I did have a pinched nerve in my spine; it was the cause for the pain and numbness in my lower back and down my legs. Then, it was recommended that I discontinue chiropractic sessions, and not wear the back brace.

I continued with physical therapy and pain management for a few more visits to see if I could strengthen my core. However, my doctor said, "I am pessimistic about your back getting any better and I am going to refer you to a neurosurgeon for consultation".

"Do I have to have surgery?"

"I can't really say", he responded. "All I know is that I have done everything I can for you and there is no improvement. This is not normal."

I left the appointment, with more medication, a referral to a neurosurgeon. "Dr. S. is a good neurosurgeon at Mount Sinai Hospital, and he accepts your insurance," he said, and handed me the prescription.

My beloved was waiting for me in the car, eager to hear the news. I could not hold back the tears as I revealed what the neurologist had said. Once I called the neurosurgeon's office, I wanted to make the earliest appointment, and was terribly disappointed to hear his appointments were two months out. Silently, I prayed that I could be squeezed into the surgeon's schedule.

His receptionist who checked his schedule to confirm a time, then said, "Oh, someone just cancelled, so I'm able to schedule you in sixteen days."

I felt relieved and very blessed. At that moment I

thanked God because I knew that this earlier appointment was a miracle; He was working for my greater good.

I could no longer tolerate the pain, couldn't even walk one block without sitting down. Moreover, walking from my door to the elevator in my building, which is about twenty feet, was a struggle.

In preparation for the consultation, I committed to focus on maintaining a positive attitude and frame of mind through meditation—while experiencing feelings of peace, ease, and my sense of being grounded.

I believed that surgery was the only thing that could help my back and my quality of life. The fear about the condition of my back, which literally felt like a bag of broken bones in need of a brace to hold them together, impacted me physically, emotionally, and spiritually, but I remained optimistic.

On February 8, 2016, we arrived for the appointment. Dr. S., a pleasant, sensitive, and compassionate looking person introduced himself and showed us the x-rays of my back on a monitor. He reiterated that it was a classic condition and many people were born with small spinal canals. He explained the procedure he felt would correct the problem.

I asked, "Is surgery the only way?"

He kindly explained how other options held little chance of improvement, and explained the laminectomy (surgery that creates space by removing the lamina—the back part of the vertebra that covers your spinal canal. Also known as "decompression surgery," it enlarges your spinal canal to relieve pressure on the spinal cord or nerves, including compression and fusion of the vertebrae in the lower back). It sounded severe, yet I knew I must do it.

Just as I was bonding with Dr. S., he said that he would refer me to a Dr. John M. Caridi. He reassured me, "I will assist with surgery. You're not getting rid of me that easily."

Miracles continued. Though I had not yet met with Dr. Caridi, his receptionist put me into his schedule right away. The Universe was working on my behalf—I felt it continuously.

I met with Dr. Caridi the following week for an evaluation. My primary diagnosis was *lumbosacral spondylosis*. Dr. Caridi confirmed that I would need a laminectomy, decompression and fusion in my back. He also explained that in my case he would put four titanium screws into certain parts of my spine, open the small canal, clear out the stenosis (arthritis) and fuse several vertebrae.

The hospital stay would be three or four days, and the incision would be four or five inches. The recovery would be six to eight weeks with total recovery in six months. It was beginning to sound hopeful.

One week after meeting with Dr. Caridi, my insurance approved the surgery for March 2, 2016. Now was the time to "Catch and Release," taught by Katye Anna Clark, to eliminate the mind chatter:

Am I making the right decision?

Have I conferred enough with God, my angels, and my spirit guides for guidance?

In my spirit, I felt confirmation that I had made the right decision—thinking to myself: *I will not allow myself to succumb to any negative thoughts which could hinder my positive energy flow for my surgery.*

Days prior to surgery seemed like an eternity. Some days I felt physically well and even thought that I may not even need to have surgery. This made me pray even harder, as

I called out to God and my angels to assure me that I had made the right decision.

On March 2, 2016, I was admitted to Mount Sinai Hospital and prepped for surgery, with the anesthesiologist fully explaining all the specifics of anesthesia and surgery. I was happy when my oldest sister arrived—I needed her support.

At that point I felt no fear, and knew that God would take care of me. With a big smile, I greeted Dr. Caridi, confidently stating, "I am ready."

After seven-and-one-half hours of surgery and time in the recovery unit, I awoke smiling when I saw my beloved and my sister looking down on me.

My family informed me that eight titanium screws and two rods were placed in my back. At first hearing this, I felt surprised and sad because I believed I would only be getting four titanium screws and no one had mentioned rods. I could not imagine having all that hardware in my back, yet I knew deep down that my back badly needed the reinforcement this offered. Later I was told by Dr. Caridi, that the eight titanium screws and two rods were placed between four sets of vertebrae from L3 to L5 and S1 with decompression and fusion, to stabilize my spine.

After four days in the hospital, I was discharged on March 6, 2016, with my walker in hand. The social worker had provided me with information to contact the Visiting Nurse Services of New York for home care services, which began on March 8, 2016.

I would receive six in-home visits from nurses, physical therapy, and have a home attendant for personal needs. This reassured me.

Two days before I was to return for my two-week follow-up with Dr. Caridi, I began to feel pain under my left breast when I breathed deeply. On that day, the physical therapist was walking with me in the hallway of my building, when I became nauseous. I returned to the apartment and regurgitated—not a good sign!

Instead of seeing Dr. Caridi, I saw his PA. After telling her of the pain under my left breast, she immediately sent me for tests, and found that there was a small pulmonary embolism in my left lung. I was readmitted to the hospital for another three days for observation, and began taking blood thinners to dissolve the blood clot. I'm very aware of how blessed I am to have paid close enough attention to my body signs—the embolism could have been deadly.

Unfortunately, I've reminded myself how, throughout the years, prior to surgery, the pain in my back worsened, and I administered home remedies without success, and over time, I became helpless. Lesson learned!

From this experience I've learned the importance of being present with your body signals, and to act quickly. I realize that self-care is a form of health care which leads to self-healing, self-love and self-compassion. Doctors are given knowledge and training for a reason, and as I am healing today, I am grateful.

Being flat on my back, totally dependent, needing help for everything humbled me. It helped me open my heart to loving and being loved—and to be cared for by others, to exercise the attitude of gratitude, to trust, and to be less self-centered.

Thank you to those of you who work in such professions—I grew in my appreciation of others who were there for me, unconditionally around the clock, as was my caregiver, Joyce. It also strengthened my faith, as I asked for and witnessed tangible help from God, angels and spirit guides.

My greater point! Don't miss out on your life because you have back problems, or other health issues. Don't procrastinate!

Like me, you want to be able to walk in the city and in the beauty of nature—walk wherever you like. Most of all, please remember, you make the most of life when you can make the most of yourself—*and that's beautiful!*

Veronica R. Lynch, Ph.D.

Healing Artist, Veronica R. Lynch, Ph.D., has twenty years of experience as a licensed clinical social worker and psychotherapist for adolescents, children and families, promoting better health and mental wellness. She is the creator of the "7 Balancing Acts for Wholeness: A Path to Revitalization." Her passion is to help others raise their life-force energy to put an end to suffering—and to replace it with a new and vital life. Veronica says, "After every storm, the sun will shine." She encourages those with whom she works to never give up on hopes and dreams. Her mission is to empower, and to help people become free of the blocks from the past that prevent experiencing a life of abundance, peace, joy, happiness and bliss. Dr. Lynch is contributing author in the international bestselling books, *Pebbles in the Pond: Wave 4* and *Wave 5*. For more information about her retreats, products and services, visit:

www.createwhole.com

vlynch@createwhole.com

"To love is to receive a glimpse of heaven."

—Karen Sunde

Postpartum Depression: From Bizarre to Blessing

JUDY DIPPEL

Our dream had come true, and at twenty-six I was going to be a mom. My husband was thrilled too, but little did we know that amidst our absolute joy, lurked a nightmare about to happen.

For me, postpartum depression appeared overnight, coming out of nowhere, stripping away the person I knew myself to be—shaking my usual confidence and "can do" attitude. Abnormal for me, I chose to suffer in silence. I told no one. Too embarrassed by the bizarre phobias that penetrated my brain involving horrible diseases; these, along with anxiety, superstitions and panic haunted me during my last trimester of pregnancy.

Little was spoken or written about postpartum depression in those days—and the broad range of symptoms that can occur, before and after birth. Now I know that those can be as simple as "baby blues," or much more extreme—with a host of issues—like anxiety, obsessive-compulsive disorder, traumatic stress disorder. And most disturbing, postpartum depression can present itself with symptoms of extreme psychosis in mother's stories, like those we are horrified to hear about in the news.

Being an optimist, but ignorant about what was happening during my initial onset of symptoms, I expected a quick fix, looking forward to my hormones, *and my mind*, returning to normal after I gave birth. It didn't work out that way. Instead, I was consumed with fear every waking hour—pretending I was *fine* to all who knew me—yet walking through a thick fog, and a scary maze that I felt had no way out—ever!

In my mind, whatever *this* was—*was permanent* with no hope of feeling *normal* again. Thinking in my phobic state: *No one would know I was physically ill with a horrible disease, but I was. I would die. I was convinced no one and nothing could ever help.*

Feeling removed from myself, I was a mere observer *of me.* And having never been depressed, I had no idea that, in itself, was a classic sign of depression. As a medical assistant, I worked in an OB-GYN practice until my daughter was born. I had thought I was well-versed in the facts and myths about pregnancy and birth. Not even close!

My search for answers would bring the facts and understanding I needed, but not quickly. Eventually I validated that postpartum depression is not a sign of weakness, or a problem due to choices made, but is clinically diagnosable, rooted in physiological cause—a bona fide, *terrifying,* clinical condition.

But during the fogginess, then, what *was totally clear* was that I had to be going crazy—literally; there was no other explanation. I felt totally unsound, falling to pieces little-by-little, day-by-day, my former secure self nowhere to be seen. I looked in the mirror and thought… *Who are you?*

It all began when I was seven months pregnant. I got the flu, became dehydrated, and had to go into the hospital to receive intravenous rehydration. It was an understatement to say, after that, I didn't feel at all like myself—physically, emotionally or mentally.

You, like most people, have probably had this experience when you wake up in the morning: As you stir awake, for the first minute or two you, feel free from anything disturbing, then reality hits like a tsunami, and concerns come crashing over you—drowning out peace of mind *and* heart, shredding away the joy you first felt at the morning light. Once concerns, or a tragic reality or circumstance hits your brain, peace-of-mind immediately vanishes.

That was me, every day my phobias and anxiety was like being stalked by a tiger, pouncing upon me, creating consuming fear—I was running for my life! The so-called tiger manifested itself in the form of a series of irrational phobias cemented in my brain, such as: *I am a mother for the first time, but I'm sure I've got multiple sclerosis and it will quickly and uncontrollably, effectively incapacitate me. No doctor will diagnose it, no one knows but me. I will die. My child will be motherless.* It was as if this destiny was inevitable. Nothing could, or would, be done to prevent it.

After my perfect and beautiful daughter was born, a mother's love was born, too. Even so, I continued to be frazzled from a growing list of physical and mental symptoms. Obviously not able to keep it to myself any longer, I sought help from every doctor who might be able to shed light. Unfortunately, all too often the different specialists chalked it up as being a new mom. (Yes, that part they had right, but if only they had also been aware of postpartum depression as a debilitating condition. But no, not even the psychiatrist

I went to seemed aware, but this was 1976.) They gave me medication for depression, anxiety, and my rapid heartbeat, which helped. For that I was grateful, but not wanting to stay on medication forever, I questioned, "What is causing this?" No one could tell me. I was an anomaly.

This went on for eighteen months before a friend brought me Dr. Robert Atkins, *Low-Carb Diet* book enlightening me to the many troublesome symptoms of hypoglycemia. I dedicated myself to his diet, and within six months I was much better, and able to go off all of the medications doctors had put me on for the phobias and anxiety, rapid heartbeat; and sweating, thirst, cravings, blurred vision, weakness, shakiness, mental confusion—the list went on. I was a mess, but thankfully for the most part I put one foot in front of the other, caring for my daughter, and able to function, though never at 100 percent.

There's more: the *really good news* and purpose of having to struggle through postpartum depression was about to make itself known to me. We had friends that cared about us—and because they did, they made a gesture that changed my life forever, and they made it possible for me to receive a gift I didn't even know existed.

It seemed simple enough: five months into what proved to be the hardest time of my life (a year before going on the Atkins diet), they invited us over for a visit to their home at Christmastime. Their Christmas tree glowed, bright with lights, as we sat eating sugar cookies and drinking tea. The scent of the apple pie that had just finished baking, fresh in the air.

I tried to shove my phobias aside, get the tiger off my back for awhile, as I made small talk—and then another couple arrived. We had not met them before, but really enjoyed getting to know them, as they were interesting, nice people. And… he, Victor, was a pastor. As the evening went on, I surprised myself when I started sharing openly about how awful I felt and what a basket case I was; I finally let it all out—(except for having told my husband and mom, and doctors.)

I had been raised a Christian, but didn't know much beyond Sunday school and sitting in the pews on Sunday morning. Now, I was about to step right up to a front-row seat!

Victor asked if we could pray about the situation. Well, I had prayed alone, but I hadn't really prayed with anyone much, so I didn't know what to expect. He explained, "God is ready and waiting for you to accept Jesus' sacrifice for you."

"It is a free gift, given by grace. You just have to believe in your heart, then reach out and take it like a precious diamond. God gives His new life generously, easily."

Vic asked readily, "Can we kneel and pray?" I felt drawn to do so and agreed. He laid his hand on my head, an experience I had never had. Honestly, I don't remember the exact words he prayed. I only remember that I had an immediate and a phenomenal experience. As he prayed, I could feel the presence of God touch me, surrounding me completely. I experienced a peace and love come from deep within, unlike anything I had ever known in my life. This was completely new to me. I'd not been around this in my life, and this *amazing grace,* was without question, God.

As I knelt, Jesus himself, his spirit, came into that room and wrapped his arms around me to *give me the greatest gift—his sweet, sweet love!* I couldn't see him with my eyes, but my spirit responded earnestly to his call, his touch. Suddenly, I knew him as the person who had come to earth and died for me—so real, so compassionate and caring. *Jesus loved me!* It wasn't just a childhood song. His love washed over me like a warm ocean wave, relaxing and soothing my frazzled spirit, body and mind.

Jesus took me by the hand and called me, yes me, "His friend and His beloved daughter," and then offered me forgiveness and love.

Fortunately, I took what God offered: *Himself.* What did it mean? I didn't know and I didn't begin to speculate. It was not an intellectual exercise or a ritual I had to figure out—on that eventful day—or today. It was newborn faith.

The physical symptoms of postpartum depression continued after that evening, but God's love diffused the fear, calmed my mind, and gave me hope and assurance that my answer would come (Dr. Atkins low-carb diet was brought to me by a friend 15 months later). The words in the Bible came to life on the page, as I grew into a closer relationship with Jesus, and applied his teachings in my life—now, for thirty-nine years.

That hard season taught me things that can help you too. First, that with life comes stressful, (sometimes feeling like more than we can bear) seasons that *we must determine to walk courageously through.* These hard times come in many shapes, sizes and severity—and take human perseverance. Second, we must be willing to open up to trusted friends or family to *seek help,* and not try to go it alone. Third, there is something more out there—more able, knowledgeable and powerful than ourselves—God. *Not just God way up in the sky, but God, Jesus Christ, and the Holy Spirit, who reaches out to each one of us as if we are the only person on earth.*

It's not about what we do, but what HE did, and continues to do today.

I know a real Jesus, the person whose Holy Spirit stands with me. I am grateful for postpartum depression, because without that desperation that drove me to my knees, I'm not sure when I would have surrendered my will to God's greater will and goodness.

I can guarantee you one thing, no two of us are dealt with in the same way as we seek and accept a personal relationship with Jesus. I encourage you to never compare your experience with God to that of others. Seek Jesus for yourself and you will find an experience specially composed and tailored—just for you! I will never get over it—why God would show himself real to me; open my eyes to him. He is faithful and always with me, whether I am wandering in the fog, or walking straight ahead on a clear and sunny day.

Wherever I am—so is God's sweet, loving presence beside me... and beside you, if you so choose!

Judy Dippel

Judy Dippel is women's inspirational author and speaker, freelance commercial writer and editor. Judy has a passion to address subjects with complete honesty—those that affect real women, with real problems, needing real solutions—of which, she says she is one! She writes and speaks on: motherhood, friendship, postpartum depression, love and relationships—as well as being a writing coach and more. In both the shared joys and universal challenges women face, Judy offers guidance, hope and encouragement. And she is the first one to admit, "I will never arrive and have it all together, *but thankfully God does.* As women, I feel we owe it to one other to share what we know and show that we care! Every day brings a fresh start and new opportunities to live out our purpose, our passions, and to positively influence our world, one person at a time." Judy is enthusiastic and transparent in her books, presentations and interviews. All her work reflects her love for people, her heart, relationship with God and her Christian faith.

judy@judydippel.com

www.jldwrites.com

Acknowledgements

Our gratitude to the twenty-one authors of this book for their contribution and their belief in us to fulfill the vision for this SPARKS series. It has been a joy-filled journey to work with each one, in our author trainings, and as this book grew into a reality. And each author holds a special place in our heart; they inspired us to fulfill our purpose, as we collaborated to expand theirs, their message and visibility.

A heartfelt thank you to our dear friend, Judy Dippel, who joined us in this vision and was far more than the editor of this book. She held our hands on many aspects of the book details and was our pillar of clarity at times. We appreciate how she sincerely supported each of our authors, helping them to relay the heart of their story, clearly, to you, the reader.

We give special thanks for the vision that Patricia Marshall of Luminare Press, our publisher, held for us. The publishing process can be more complex than imagined, but her personal and professional interest simplified the process. Her commitment is deeply appreciated, and to be commended...and now on to the next edition.

And Catherine Van Wetter, we thank her for interviewing each of our authors, offering them an opportunity to share more of who they are through audio recordings. For some, it was their first interview, and Catherine made the process "a comfortable conversation" they could take part in with confidence, helping them hone their skills for further story and book promotion.

We appreciate, and must acknowledge our families for their unconditional love and support. Their patience and willingness to listen to our continual stream of ideas…is invaluable!

And finally, we thank all of the visionaries and change makers that have entrusted us to support them over the past several years. You are the inspiration that seeded this vision. You know who you are …

A New Era of Story Sharing is Born

We are taking applications for Life SPARKS, Edition #2

Our SPARKS book series is publishing stories that illuminate, inspire and ignite hearts

Your Story Matters. You Matter!

Learn how you can participate in our SPARKS program and have your story published in a SPARKS book. Learn why you should.

Our professionals manage the details. You receive the beauty of learning from us, as you live your publishing dream.

- **Connect** with our SPARKS team to chat about what you would attempt to write… if you could! With the help of a professional team, find out how you can!
- **Inquire** about the author training provided with your SPARKS experience.
- **Gain** knowledge and skills through an experiential, proven program and author bonus benefits.

Email contact: Team@AuthenticMessengers.com

Link to create appointment: www.AuthenticMessengers.com/share-my-spark

Visit these websites for more information:

www.AuthenticMessengers.com

www.facebook.com/authenticmessengers

Meet The SPARKS Team
Your Success Is Our Success

Tami Blodgett

Co-Creator SPARKS Program
CEO Global Visibility LLC
www.AuthenticMessengers.com
www.GlobalVisibilityLLC.com

Tami is a respected "Business Strategist," who tirelessly serves those who yearn to make a real difference in the world. Have a brainstorm session with Tami—you'll see—there's no going back!

"Supporting changemakers to discover their purpose, share their message and build a thriving business on the foundation of their values is my expertise and passion."

Denise Beins

Co-Creator SPARKS Program,
COO Global Visibility LLC,
www.AuthenticMessengers.com
www.GlobalVisibilityLLC.com

Denise consults and professionally guides visionaries and entrepreneurs in how to keep their business visible, thriving and efficient.

"I am passionate about efficiency, strategies and functional management."

214

Judy Dippel

SPARKS Editor
Owner of JLD Writes
www.JLDwrites.com

Judy is the author of several books, inspirational speaker, ghostwriter, writing coach, and owner of a freelance writing business.

"My role is to collaborate with authors, help bring their story to life, to influence and inspire readers."

Patricia Marshall

SPARKS Publisher
Owner of Luminare Press
www.LuminarePress.com

Patricia brings a thorough knowledge of printing and a passion for non-fiction book editing to the process.

"I have a strong desire to help authors produce a polished, professional book, while they learn more about the publishing industry."